LONE WORKING
Personal Safety
A guidebook for health & social care workers

Lone Worker Personal Safety
A guidebook for health & social care workers

By Gerard O'Dea
Dynamis Insight 2014

Details about our training and advisory services are available at
www.dynamis-insight.com

Office Telephone: (UK +44) (0)844 812 9795
Email: **info@dynamis-insight.com**

Our Lone Worker Training Course information
and supplementary materials for this book are available at
www.lone-working.com

LONE WORKING
PERSONAL SAFETY

A guidebook for health & social care workers

Gerard O'Dea

Contents

About the Author

Gerard O'Dea is a Personal Safety, Conflict Management and Physical Interventions Training Consultant and Director and Principal Trainer at Dynamis Insight in the UK. www.dynamis-insight.com

University of Stirling BA Business Studies and Japanese Cardiff University Law School / Bond Solon Certified Expert Witness (Criminal Cases)

National Federation for Personal Safety (NFPS) *Accredited Instructor*

National Federation for Personal Safety (NFPS) *Licensed Centre for Delivery of BTEC Awards*

National Federation for Personal Safety (NFPS) *Certified Violence at Work Risk Assessor*

BTEC Level 4 Professional Award in *Preparing to Teach in the Lifelong Learning Sector* (PTLLS)

BTEC Level 3 Advanced Award in *Delivery of Conflict Management Training*

BTEC Level 3 Advanced Award in Advanced Self Defence Instruction

BTEC Level 3 Advanced Award in *Physical Restraint Practice*

BTEC Level 3 Advanced Award in *Coaching & Instruction of Physical Restraint*

BTEC Level 3 Advanced Award in *Safe and Effective use of Restraint Devices*
BTEC Level 3 Advanced Award in Physical Intervention (SIA)

CIEH Level 3 Award in *Principles and Practice of Risk Assessment*
Certified at the NHS *National Conflict Resolution syllabus Familiarisation Seminar*
Certified at the AELE Workshop on *Legal, Psychological and Biomechanical Aspects of Officer-Involved Lethal and Less-Lethal Use of Force.*

Speaker:
Protecting Scottish Public Services Workers National Conference Glasgow (2007)
Control & Restraint General Services Association National Conference Edinburgh (2010)

I have delivered training in personal safety, conflict risk management and physical intervention for over 150 organisations and frequently provide professional consultation and advice on:

- Human Factors-based Training Needs Analysis and Programme Design

- Psychological and Physiological factors in high-risk violent confrontations

- The issues in common and criminal law in relation to use of force

- How the Human Rights Act 1998 impacts on training and management of violence

- How Health and Safety legislation relates to staff who face occupational violence

- Restraint-related risks of sudden death and excited delirium

- Obligations of managers under the Management of Health and Safety at Work Regulations 1999

- The impact of legislation and national guidance for the care of vulnerable people in crisis

My client list includes the Scottish Prison Service College, Police Services, HM Courts Service, the State Hospital at Carstairs, NHS Primary Care trusts, Local Authority Health & Social Care Departments, Social Housing Organisations, the Brain Injury Trust, Four Seasons Healthcare, Health Authority Abu Dhabi and Dubai Healthcare Authority in addition to hundreds of private care providers, community teams, security providers and educational institutions across the UK.

Acknowledgements

To my wife Vanessa, who endures my constant travel and absences as I travel every road, railway, and at times, airway in the UK and internationally in the pursuit of knowledge and people who need this knowledge. She is always supportive, understanding, and when necessary, she challenges me to go one step further.

Essential guides in my own quest have been Mr. Mark Dawes of the National Federation for Personal Safety (NFPS), for his illumination of the legalities of occupational violence risk management and his constancy with advice at the end of a telephone. Mark's work on 'Understanding Reasonable Force' was an essential key—a Rosetta stone—which unlocked so many of the issues discussed here.

On the other side of the pond, Mr. Tony Torres of Conflict Resolution Professionals (9atitudes.com) has consistently offered patient, succinct insights into human behaviour in conflict which have been a constant touchstone. Tony's "9 attitudes" framework is the backbone of the personal safety advice in this book.

Over the years the support of my professional colleagues, Ms. Spencer and Mr. Glover, has been heartening, and their companionship on our training projects has allowed so many insights to mature with their input.

Finally, I would like to thank the thousands of lone-working staff I have met over the years during our explorations in this area of personal safety. Your penetrating questions, realisations, investigations, experiments and dogged endeavours in an effort to stay safe have shaped and molded every word in this book.

Gerard O'Dea

Foreword by Mark Dawes

Director, National Federation for Personal Safety

Lone working is a hazardous activity that places many people at risk of abuse, threatening behaviour and violence. This can result in staff being left emotionally, mentally and physically vulnerable and harmed. Some have even been killed. Yet still today, many staff, be they directly employed, part time or self-employed, are left to work on their own or in isolation without any proper safeguards in place in terms of advice, guidance, formal training or equipment.

This not only leaves staff vulnerable, but the employer vulnerable, too, and there are many cases of organisations having been prosecuted for failing to uphold their duty of care to their staff or others. Today, with the inclusion of the Corporate Manslaughter and Corporate Homicide Act now firmly established in UK law, and cases rising exponentially each year, employers can find themselves prosecuted and even sent to prison should a member of staff or someone else die through a lone working activity that was not properly risk-managed.

In essence, if nothing is done about the risks involved in lone working, it is a no-win situation for the staff, the organisation, its management teams, and even the service users who will suffer if prosecutions and fines result in valuable services being withdrawn or cut back.

Yet, the strange thing is that a lot can be done, and it can be done very easily for a very reasonable and practicably justified investment. But if this is so, why isn't it being done?

There are a number of reasons: lack of time, lack of resources, lack of interest and because of conformity and complacency—accepting things as they are. Some employers and even some staff accept risk as part of the job; the reasons given for not doing something are mere excuses. However, whatever the excuse may be, these reasons could be seen by a court of law as evidence of negligence in failing to keep a worker safe and even a criminal act.

And there are not just legal reasons for managing personal safety; there are also moral and ethical ones. Many staff who work alone or in isolation do so to help others. They provide a service to the vulnerable, and they are willing to take the risk because if they didn't perhaps the job would not get done. But that just isn't a reason for ignoring safety—by employee or employer.

Recently, a Supreme Court ruling has given families of soldiers killed in action leave to sue the Ministry of Defence for negligence in failing to provide these soldiers with adequate equipment and training, which the family members believe resulted in them dying. These soldiers went to war and were prepared to make the ultimate sacrifice. But isn't it somewhat perverse that they were killed, not by the enemy, but by a failure in the duty of care owed to them by their own side. That is wrong on all levels. The "old guard attitude," where accepting the risk as "part of the job," is dead in the water and provides no defence.

Keeping people safe isn't just a legal obligation, it is a humanitarian one. In this modern era where technology and information is so advanced, the ability to keep people safe is not beyond any employer's means, especially if the employers can be shown how to use that knowledge, information and technology in an efficient and functional way. That is what the author, Gerard O'Dea, offers in this book.

Everyone has the right to go home in the same way that they arrived at work. Safely. That is not only our obligation to those we employ, it is our duty to ensure it.

Today the word "stress" is used to describe all things that one cannot cope with, and all employers are now obliged legally to ensure that their staff are not "suffering from stress in the workplace." What is not commonly known is that one of the biggest causes of "stress" is "learned helplessness"—giving up and accepting defeat. This can be a danger, because some people stop caring and accept whatever fate awaits them. They become complacent and conform to accepting less than what they are worth. Then the risk simply becomes "part of the job," and we are back in a no-win situation.

Here is your chance to do the right thing simply because it is the right thing to do—on all levels. The advice in this book will not only keep you and your team safe, it will help to alleviate stress in the workplace, making your team more productive, thus allowing them to provide the services that are so valuable to so many.

As a responsible person, the advice in this book will give you a stronger defence to any challenge for negligence and/or a prosecution and, more importantly, it will give you peace-of-mind in assuring that someone else's son, daughter, mother and/or father can go home to their family every evening. Money can't buy that.

Mark Dawes

Director, NFPS Ltd

Foreword by Mark Williams

Director, Tactical Safety Responses Ltd

There is a legal obligation for organisations to keep their staff safe at work, and a lone worker for the purposes of this guidance is defined as someone who works on their own with no close or direct supervision.

Lone working is not where individuals experience transient situations in which they find themselves alone, but where individuals are knowingly and foreseeably placed in circumstances in which they undertake work activities without direct or close supervision.

This book explores the numerous pieces of Law & Legislation that employers should adhere to. However in my experience this legislation is often quoted after the event, and when someone has been injured! The Law is the Law, and it is there is protect people, and not up for debate, but I want to keep this foreword simple and straight forward, and in way that the readers can relate to.

Personal Safety Training as a general heading can involve lots of subjects and headings, but in relation to the safety of a person, it is important to think about all the foreseeable things that could go wrong and plan as best as we can to prevent them....this is the basic assumption of risk assessment.

I open a lot of courses on this matter by posing a simple question in relation to personal safety:

If a loved one was away on holiday, or out for the night, and didn't return on time, at what point would you get worried?

Being organised in your personal life reduces stress and better prepares you and your family for risks, and it is no different for lone workers and the above question is also relevant in the work place. If someone is working alone, at what point would you be worried about them and what could happen to them?

Quite often you could read an article relating to personal safety, and in 'hindsight' a couple of simple common sense control measures would arguably have changed the outcome.

For our personal safety, or the personal safety of an employee to be compromised, there generally needs to be the following present: a Victim, an Aggressor and an Opportunity. By taking simple common sense steps (assessing the foreseeable risks) we can help reduce the 'Opportunity'

As mentioned the Law, together with Staff Safety Policies and Risk Assessments should keep staff safe first, and the requirement for the use of physical force should be a last resort.

However if the risk assessment identifies that it is foreseeable that a person may have to resort to defending themselves or another, then it is important that the training is based on techniques that work and takes into consideration all the research that has been done into the stress of confrontation, and not just ticks an organisational box.

The stress and aftermath of a physical confrontation can be very stressful and have lasting effects. This book explores the chronological route to protect lone workers by explaining and identifying the legislation and legal issues together with explaining the stress and effects to an individual during confrontation.

It is a must read for anyone responsible for the safety of their staff

As a footnote remember this:

"That man is an aggressive creature will hardly be disputed. With the exception of certain rodents, no other vertebrate habitually destroys members of its own species. No other animal takes positive pleasure in the exercise of cruelty upon another of his own kind. We generally describe the most repulsive of mans' cruelty as brutal or bestial, implying by these adjectives that such behaviour is characteristic of less highly developed animals than ourselves.

In truth, however, the extremes of brutal behaviour are confined to man and there is no parallel in nature to our savage treatment of each other. The sombre fact is that we are the cruellest and most ruthless species to have ever walked the earth."

STORR - HUMAN AGGRESSION 1968

Mark Williams
Director – Tactical Safety Responses Ltd

Chapter 1:
Preface

As I sat down to write the introduction to this book, I looked up at the shelves over my desk and took a quick inventory. There, on a shelf otherwise crammed with texts on conflict management, use-of-force law, psychology, physiology, social care issues and threat assessment, are 11 handwritten notebooks. For the past 8 years I have taken an A4 notebook to every training session I have conducted, and noted down the key points which came up during the sessions.

These notebooks contain stories collected by asking thousands of staff who have faced situations to retell their stories and share them, so that others who have yet to face those dangers can learn the lessons they uncovered. I am priviliged to be able to create this guidebook—a distillation of the recounting of those survival stories.

My best guess is that you are reading this book because you want to understand your own risk of facing real violence and aggression at work. You want to know how to avoid dangerous situations, how to de-escalate aggressive people if you can't avoid them, or you want to be able to deal with them effectively and protect yourself if absolutely necessary. If not for yourself, then you wonder how you might help those you are responsible for—people in your team, your department or your organisation.

Having had the opportunity during hundreds of training sessions in the past 8 years with healthcare, social care and community-based professionals and private citizens who were looking for this resilience in the face of threats to their safety, and listening to their experiences of the challenges they have faced, and having discussed the ideas set out in this book, I believe that we can encourage greater resilience in the face of adversity—specifically for lone workers facing the threat of violence.

My deep involvement in personal safety started about fifteen years ago when I was asked a seemingly simple but ultimately very challenging question. A young woman who was learning martial arts from me was nearing her black-belt grading exam. She and her partner stopped me during a training session on self-defence techniques—all of us standing there in our traditional white pyjamas—and asked whether the techniques she was studying would actually work if she ever needed them, for real, down the proverbial 'dark alley.'

I tried then to offer those young women the best and most honest answer I could. That question, asked directly that day by them but left unsaid by many of the other learners I met in that environment, sparked a journey that I am still on today.

I knew there was more to her question than just whether a twist of a wrist could release a hold, or whether a strike could distract; there were deeper issues at hand. Firstly, there was a motivational issue—would she be able to summon the mental strength, the resilience, to persevere in a difficult moment? Next were issues about the chaotic mobile geometry of a physical confrontation—all those collisions and sudden movements and off-balancings which occur and how to prepare for them?

In the first instance, how on earth did she get into a situation where physical protection was required?

The questions, when I looked further into the issue, went deeper and deeper.

My company name, Dynamis, came into being one day while reading one of my favourite authors: Steven Pressfield. In a novel where he explored issues of motivation, self-belief and the difficulty of overcoming overwhelming odds, he wrote that:

"Those who do not understand war believe it contention between armies, friend against foe. No. Rather friend and foe duel as one against an unseen antagonist, whose name is Fear... What drives the soldier is cardia, heart, and dynamis, the will to fight. Nothing else matters"

Dynamis—the will, motivation, perseverance and resilience needed to survive a confrontation, would form the cornerstone of our advice and training in good personal safety practice and physical tactics.

Lone workers have told us many stories over the years of the various situations they have been in where they felt their safety was threatened when working alone with vulnerable or at-risk people. If you are an experienced lone worker then there is a good chance that you have experienced one or number of instances of feeling threatened during your career:

- While in the community working alone, you met a client or other person who physically threatened you—a physical assault.

- You have experienced verbal aggression or you felt "strange" or "inappropriate" behaviour from clients, which made you worry for your safety.

- For some reason not immediately clear to you, you got a bad feeling or began to feel concerned in a situation before anything bad had happened. (We refer to this as the "heebie-jeebie" moment!)

As evidenced by surveys and statistics (for example from the Royal College of Nursing Lone Working Surveys in 2007 and 2011), the risks faced by lone workers in health and social care can include:

- Verbal aggression from frustrated service users or others.

- Physical violence from aggressive service users or others.

- Being isolated and contained in a room or building against their will.

In a group of a dozen or more experienced social or healthcare lone workers, for example, I would find it quite normal for at least one worker to relate a story about being trapped or detained by a person they visited; at least one story about a physical assault; at least one story about a weapon being present during an interaction; and quite a few stories about verbal aggression from the person they visited.

Some workers find it easy to laugh off these incidents. Some workers struggle with the memory, often noting that it made them change their working practices. Others are visibly affected with the fear, uncertainty and isolation they felt in their moment of crisis in their client's front room, bathroom, bedroom or hallway.

As we will see later, everyone is "wired up" differently for aggression, violence and fear. Situations which would stop one person from ever going back to their workplace might be laughed off by another. A person's upbringing, experiences, professional training and life-lessons in resilience will also to a large extent decide which kind of aftermath each survivor experiences.

In Chapter 2 I will introduce a basic framework for shaping your thinking about personal safety, one which I will expand on later when we explore the changing phases and states involved in a violent incident, in Chapter 5.

In Chapter 3 I will explore the requirements of health and safety law in the UK and the obligations it places on the employers of lone workers. I will particularly focus this exploration on the issues raised by the risks of violence and aggression towards lone workers. While we are discussing risk-control methods, I want to discuss Lone Worker safety devices with you in Chapter 4. These new technologies show huge promise and are a welcome addition to the control of risks, however I will discuss their place in the range of options available.

Chapter 6 deals with aggression triggers and behavioural influence—the concept of de-escalation of aggression through behavioural and verbal, non-physical means. I hope to explore a rule-of-thumb model for diagnosing triggers and which can be used to prescribe behaviours which assist the de-escalation to happen.

Following on from this, in Chapter 7, I will address the non-verbal communication involved in inter-personal confrontations and how this can—and in my opinion should—become a habitual behaviour which enhances safety for a lone worker. The effective management of proximity in the close confines of a front room, bedroom or bathroom can offer more time for de-escalation.

In Chapter 8 we will deal with the decision-making and legal principles which come into play when the de-escalation tactics fail and the aggression turns to violence. The lone worker sometimes needs to protect herself, and so we must enable her with a robust and legally sound decision-making framework based on the concept of 'Reasonable Force.'

In Chapter 9 I will attempt to distill general personal safety principles which contain practical, positive advice for any person to improve their safety and their preparedness for dealing with the kinds of situations described throughout the rest of the material in this book.

'Mortui Vivos Docent'
Within this book are many examples of how things can go wrong and how things can sometimes end tragically. My course attendees sometimes question me about why I use these "negative" examples during my training courses—incidents where perhaps the lone worker did not go home to their family afterwards. I acknowledge and understand the reluctance of some social and healthcare staff to accept that these incidents happen, *but they do happen.*

I am a personal safety trainer. My role is to enable you to think effectively and efficiently about your personal safety. My passion and my mission is to make sure that after we have interacted—whether through this book or through a training event or in some other way—you are better enabled to make decisions which will directly affect your safety.

The "scary stories" offer us lessons. Mortui Vivos Docent means "the dead teach the living," and it is a term often used in medical schools to emphasise that we must study pathology to understand cures. It is for this reason that from time to time I will ask you to examine a real-life story of a personal safety incident which went tragically wrong for a healthcare or social-care worker—so that we may respect their memory and learn any lessons which their tragedy presents to us.

At times what is written here may challenge your beliefs about your role, about your personal approach to violence, about your interactions with others and about how you perform under survival stress.

My primary goal with this book is to give you practical advice which will inform, and I hope, enhance your decision making. My secondary goal is to inform the discussions you have within your team about how you, as a group, can better manage personal safety issues.

For these reasons, this is not a very academic book, although I have referenced almost 30 other works in the fields of communication, negotiation, aggression management, human behaviour, brain function, personal safety, threat assessment, use of force law, combat psychology, motor skill performance and stress and so on. I like to think of this book as a conversation about personal safety we might have over a cup of coffee during a break.

During this chat, I want to introduce waypoints which can guide your own decisions along a more informed path.

Speaking of being more informed, I have also included at the end of each chapter a list of recommended reading for those wishing to look closer at the evidence base or background to many of the ideas I have put forward or connections I have tried to make between scientific discoveries, behaviour and personal safety in practice. While not academically referenced in the orthodox way, I hope that the inclusion of these references will help my more curious readers to search for themselves and discover their own connections or merely review mine.

Chapter 2:

The Personal Safety Framework

Alertness, Prevention and Survival

While there are many different states or attitudes which we can bring to personal safety, and all of them can be equally important in an overall strategy for dealing with violence and aggression, I want to now introduce you to just three of them. We are going to look at the Alert, Preventive and Engagement attitudes to get you thinking about personal safety as a series of connected and sometimes overlapping phases. This book is organised around these three major phases, so you need to know what they represent!

The Alert Attitude
This first phase I want you to consider is being alert and sensitive to tricky situations which may arise. I want you to be making considerable efforts to try to detect potentially dangerous scenarios in your work and home life as far away in distance and in time from them as possible, and then using the time and space this allows to devise sensible precautions.

Formally, this means that the organisation you work for must exercise the obligations placed on them by occupational, health and safety at work laws and the associated regulations and guidance.

Informally—and crucially—where the formal health and safety systems in place have failed to predict and address an emerging

risk to your safety, you must allow yourself the personal autonomy use your *alert attitude* and to weigh and consider unfolding situations and make good decisions about your safety.
Sometimes you must make these decisions in fluid and dynam-
ic scenarios.

Give yourself permission to formulate your own best strategies
to stay safe, based on what instinctively feels right in the decisive moment. Allow and give permission to your colleagues to
do this also. Ultimately, we are each responsible for assessing
and managing our own safety, but we can all be influenced by
our peers.

The Preventive Attitude
If you are exercising awareness and doing your best to be alert
to and prevent dangerous situations, then you will be successful
in avoiding almost all of them. My guess is that you are already
doing quite a bit of this! However, it is when your avoidance
strategies fail (for whatever reasons) that your preparation,
psychologically, emotionally and practically, will become crucial.

In a client's front room, when they lose control of some angry
emotions or feelings of frustration and begin to focus on you as
a target, you should now be operating decisively in the *preventive* attitude. Your goal in this moment is to prevent the evolv-
ing situation from becoming a serious threat to you.

We sometimes refer to this in our training sessions as the "Oh
Shit!" moment, when the gravity of the situation really takes
hold. In this decisive moment, when the person you are interacting with presents a danger to you, it is through your behaviour, your carefully constructed communication and your sound

tactical decisions, that you will reduce the potential for the situation to cause you harm.

Faced with a suddenly upset service user, for example, who is now presenting threatening behaviour towards you, it will be as John Monaghan stated:

"The reaction of a potential victim of violence may distinguish a verbal altercation from a murder."

- DeBecker, G, *The Gift of Fear*, 140

Standing in the client's front room, having somehow, someway, become the focus of aggression, you must think and act quickly to recognise the change in temperature of the interaction, discover the triggering stimulus and then work, through your mindful behaviour, to prevent a full escalation into violence.

Later in this book, I will offer you a framework for understanding the triggers for such aggression and the ways in which you can attempt to influence a person's behaviour.

The Survival Attitude
Your efforts to defuse and disengage during the Prevention phase may be successful—if so, excellent work! It is a delicate and risky proposition, perhaps why we like to use the word "defusing" to describe it, alluding to the work of the bomb-squad who must open up suspicious packages which could go horribly "bang" at any moment.

If your efforts to defuse this situation are unsuccessful, and the person you are working with continues to escalate through the phases of aggression and becomes enraged to the point of physical violence, then I want you to be prepared to to survive.

As an aside, it might be important to also note that you may be faced with what Rory Miller calls "asocial violence," which is violence based on resources and is not dependent on any points of negotiation or conflict normally associated with social or healthcare work. In this case you might be facing a person who sees you as only a target, a source of some resource (drugs, money, sex or other gratification) and who cannot or will not engage with your needs as a person. This 'resource preadtor' does not recognise you as a person. This is generally a far more serious and potentially harmful scenario.

In either scenario, whether through a failure in negotiation or a failure in removing your perceived value as a target, you need to be prepared now to survive by physically protecting yourself from attack.

Importantly, the law allows any person to use force to protect themselves or another person against physical violence. Contrary to popular myth, social care, community-based or healthcare workers are not excluded from this legal right!

Often for those healthcare workers who took seriously the Hippocratic oath to "Do No Harm" or those who work tirelessly in their service users' "Best Interests," the rapid decision-making which is needed to employ force decisively to survive and reverse a physical assault may be clouded by emotional inhibitions.

Care workers in particular are susceptible to erroneous beliefs about their rights to protect themselves and to prevent their clients coming to harm. "Staff who protect themselves and use force with a service user get fired" is the wildly popular but erroneous urban myth that you may have heard at some point in your career.

This myth is usually derived from popular media stories, or those passed on at coffee breaks which tell of adult safeguarding training courses in which they convince care staff that protective acts lie somewhere in a grey area and will most likely land them in hot water. In a later chapter I will tell you about the rules which govern your right to protect yourself and your service user.

These three domains—Alertness, Prevention and Survival—form the basic structure of this book and offer us a framework through which I hope to offer you greater clarity on the issues of lone worker personal safety.

Alertness and Avoidance

Awareness of the Issue
This is a list compiled by Ray Braithwaite in his book *Managing Aggression* about Social Care Staff murdered in a 25-year period from 1984:

1984: Isabel Schwartz. SOCIALWORKER. Bexley

1985 Norma Morris. SOCIAL WORKER. Haringey

1986 FrancisBetteridge. SOCIAL WORKER. Birmingham

1988 Audrey Johnson. SOCIAL WORKER. London

1992 Katie Sullivan. VOLUNTARY WORKER. Kingston-upon-Thames

1993 Georgina Robinson.OCUPATIONAL THERAPIST. Devon

1993 Jonathan Newby.VOLUNTARY WORKER. Oxford

1998 Jenny Morrison.SOCIAL WORKER. Wandsworth

1984 Isabel Schwartz. SOCIAL WORKER. Bexley

1985 Norma Morris. SOCIAL WORKER. Haringey

1986 FrancisBetteridge.SOCIAL WORKER. Birmingham

1988 Audrey Johnson. SOCIAL WORKER. London

1992 KatieSullivan.VOLUNTARY WORKER. Kingston-upon-Thames

1993 Georgina Robinson.OCUPATIONAL THERAPIST. Devon

1993 Jonathan Newby.VOLUNTARY WORKER. Oxford

1998 Jenny Morrison.SOCIAL WORKER. Wandsworth

2006 Ashleigh Ewing.SOCIAL WORKER. Newcastle

2007 Sarah Merritt.CARE WORKER. Southampton

2008 Phillip Ellison.SOCIAL WORKER. Preston

One of the difficult things I must do, as your personal safety trainer, is to make you aware that these incidents have happened. Remember, my role as your personal safety guide is to highlight the realities for you. I want to help you to protect yourself against these types of incidents happening to you or within your team. Let's examine the lessons.

Avoidance

Let us first turn our attention to a Royal College of Nursing study, published in 2007 (and updated in 2011 with similar results), which dealt with the issues of lone working and personal safety. The survey was very comprehensive and asked approximately 1500 UK nurses who work in the community about their experiences.

Let's pick out a few of the more salient points:

- 10% of the respondents had been physically assaulted at work during the two years prior to the survey.

- Only one in five staff said that their employers *always* knew their whereabouts on a given day.

- Only 18.3 percent carried out a risk assessment on their first visit, with 19.3 percent conducting a risk assessment on every visit.

- About two-thirds of respondents said that they *rarely*, *never* or only *sometimes* were provided with adequate information on referral.

- 8% of physical assaults were never reported to a line manager. 75% of physical assaults were not reported to the police.

- 25% of respondents felt unsafe at work in the previous 12 months.

Some home care staff might visit up to 14 people in one day while they are at work. I have met more than one Home Care worker who does in excess of 20 visits per day.

My first question to Lone Workers is always: **"If I walked in to your supervisor's office one day while you are out at work and asked, 'Where is Mary right now, and is she safe?' what quality of answer would I get?"** Answers vary widely.

Criminal Justice teams tend to be very aware of the risk their workers may face. Home Care staff tend to be left to their own schedule management.

Teams manage their whereabouts using a variety of methods. In/out boards are particularly common, but they are also subject to varying levels of consistency and monitoring.

Using an in/out board, workers write down their itinerary for the day noting who they are visiting and when, and what time they expect to finish the visit. People at the office can check the board and then make a phone call to confirm the person's whereabouts and safety.

When staff are asked if they ever receive "just checking to see if you're okay" phone calls, though, it becomes obvious that time pressure and other demands can make this system a less-dependable, less-robust one.

Workers sometimes visit with their clients out of hours. Visits happen all the way up to 10 pm and beyond.This means that there may be no one at the office to actually check the in/out board. Perhaps the receptionist or administrative support person leaves at 4 pm. Perhaps there is an on-call manager but she/he is only to be called in emergencies.

The common joke we hear from staff—hiding a dark reality— is that the alarm would only be raised when their family is sitting around their dinner table, "wondering where that woman who cooks dinner is?"

The burning question is, **"Are you supervising the work that is going on in your team adequately, and is the system you have put in place robust?"** Which as we shall see, could quite rightly be keeping those responsible for managing teams awake at night.

Another way to explain the same problem, perhaps in less stark terms, is to ask: "If one of your lone worker colleagues feels unwell, faints and collapses in a client's home, then when does your team find out that she needs help, and how?" If the answer is not a comprehensive one, and one that workers and managers can have confidence in, then it may be time to review and tighten your team's systems of supervision and monitoring.

Recently an entire industry has matured in order to support the responsibilities of managers in adequately supervising lone working teams. Electronic devices using mobile phone and messaging technology, GPS tracking, process management software and British Standard compliant alarm-receiving call centres are now available in subscription packages; these devices and services can significantly increase the level of supervision and support encapsulated within a safe system of lone worker safety. I will discuss this issue in a later chapter specifically devoted to Lone Worker Safety Devices.

Recording and Sharing Information

Past history of violent behaviour is the strongest predictor of future violence.

I recall reading a news article in a Sunday paper some years ago which described a reporter's experiences while spending a weekend on the road with a London Ambulance Service (LAS) crew. Amongst descriptions of paramedics being shot and being shot at and about the violence and aggression he witnessed against these staff, the reporter mentioned a very special list of addresses which was being maintained by LAS.

The journalist mentioned the existence of a list of 2,000 "high-risk" addresses in the London area which, if the emergency services are called and an ambulance is required to attend those addresses, certain precautions were to be taken. The paramedic crew was to stop on the way to the location of the emergency and put on their stab-proof vests. On arrival, they were to wait and ensure a police escort before entering into the address.

It makes sense for the LAS to take precautions—an ambulance worker is attacked in London every day of the year.

However, if you were visiting clients in the London area, would you want to know if the address on your task list today was one of those addresses?

A criminal justice social worker, or a district nurse, or a children's dental worker, for example, would probably want to know that this list was being shared with his/her team—just in case they were asked to visit one of these addresses by themselves.

Practice differs, though. One local authority we have worked with keeps a definitive record of potentially adverse violent or aggressive behavior that their staff has encountered and marks them on its database of service users. They do this in line with the NHS's (National Health Service) published guidance on Violence Warning Markers and share the information with others who may need it.

The NHS guidance, published in 2010, makes clear that information pertaining to past, and therefore potential future violence by service users, can be recorded and shared in certain broad circumstances and in line with the Data Protection Act's principles and purpose.

However, I am also aware of one local authority who burned their entire violence warning marker database in response to a perceived legal threat about breach of confidentiality or privacy. Unsurprisingly, when I ask care staff if they would want to work for that organisation, they tend to show reluctance!

Some disagree with Violence Warning Markers, stating the need for care workers to be non-judgemental, to respect diversity and equality. Of course this is a legitimate (and lawful) aim; however, respecting diversity is more appropriate to issues of race, gender, ethnicity and other areas where bias is socially unacceptable. Being non-judgmental is perfectly appropriate to issues of lifestyle, relationships, culture and choice.

Some even state that warning a care worker about a service user's history of violence will make them over-cautious and therefore *cold* or *wary* towards the client, tempting them to *pre-judge* the client.

These arguments, while well meant, cannot stand serious scrutiny in the face of the levels of violence and aggression being recorded against health and social care staff.

We must hold one key and overriding public interest in our minds: the protection of life. If that high-minded idea doesn't sound practical, then it is important to note the overriding directive of Article 2 of the Human Rights Act 1998, to which every facet of government is beholden to:

"Everyone's right to life shall be protected by law."

Furthermore, Article 2 is now supported practically by legislation such as the Corporate Manslaughter Act. Even the UK Ministry of Defence, in charge of the most professional, hard-charging combat servicemen and women in the world, is being seriously challenged on its obligations and duty to plan, control and provision its activities in such a way as to protect and safeguard life under human rights law.

Ideas of confidentiality are important but not as important as ideas about people's basic right to be protected from foreseeable risks that might put their life at risk or kill them.

Reporting Issues

Another important issue raised by the RCN survey is that about one in ten physical assaults against lone working staff in the community were not being reported to a line manager, and that 75% were not being reported to the police.

The risk of non-reporting or under-reporting is that one worker's experience of being "shoved out the door of the house" becomes the next person's punch in the face, becomes the next persons....well, who knows?

Certainly, if you or your colleagues don't feel the duty and obligation to report all the assaults that are happening "out there," then there is a crucially important element of the awareness and avoidance phase being missed-out.

You and your colleagues should feel the responsibility of protecting other co-workers and colleagues who interact with your clients. If a client has assaulted you, then it is likely—foreseeable, even—that the client could assault another worker when they go to visit with them. There would seem to be a clear moral duty to warn others of the danger, not to mention a more legal "duty of care" (see the chapter herein on health and safety obligations).

Sometimes, over years of practice, staff who start their career with a keen sense of needing to record and share this kind of information have it worn down and blunted. They have written the incident reports, discussed issues with their line managers and awaited the directives to come back down the chain of responsibility, often to no result. After repeatedly experiencing the extra work involved in reporting, but not seeing any output from their reports, eventually they ask, "Why should I spend the time to write reports when those reports aren't being acted upon?" Complacency sets in and apathy results.

Organisationally, there is a benefit to making the reporting process short, concise and easy to access. Too often the manager becomes the guardian of the mystical incident report form!

Another reason for lack of reporting can be that staff becomes convinced that being assaulted is part of their daily-expected work, and therefore does not warrant special mention in an incident report. Sometimes, too, we have become aware of managers coercing staff to not report certain incidents because of the paperwork generated or how the incident report will negatively impact the perceptions others have of their service.

Worse still, upon receiving a report of an incident occurring, the manager initiates an interview with the worker about how they must have been at fault for causing the service user to be so aggressive! This will not encourage objective reporting!

Until we are supervising workers adequately, putting safe systems of work in place, recording and sharing information about danger, treating the problem seriously and having adult discussions about risk, then we won't be able to stop the tragedies from happening. I now want explore one of these tragedies with you in order to find some meaning and value in it, with the hope that its lessons will become useful.

May 19th 2006

A 22-year old recent graduate, on her last day of a six-month internship with a mental health charity, went to visit her client, Ronald Dixon, on May 19th 2006. Within a couple of hours of her leaving the office, Dixon was at his local police station reporting her murder and turning himself in. He had stabbed her over 30 times in the living room of his home.

Ronald Dixon was a paranoid schizophrenic with a history of serious violence. He had attacked his parents with a hammer, breaking it into pieces. He had recently appeared outside Buckingham Palace, threatening to kill the Queen.

In the weeks leading up to this killing, he had been displaying increasingly erratic behaviour, including refusing the prescribed medication for his mental illness. According to neighbours, he had been drinking heavily, disappearing for days at a time and was withdrawn.

He had admitted stress about his finances. In the weeks leading up to the murder, he had attacked and broken open a pay telephone in his supported housing to get the money out of it.

The young female worker had begun working with Dixon some five months earlier, initially shadowing a more experienced colleague on her visits with him. On May 19th, she was tasked with delivering a letter to Dixon, asking him to pay for the damage he had caused inside the flat.

He turned on her and stabbed her over thirty times. He then calmly walked his dog to the police station and handed himself in.

At the subsequent trial, his barrister said, "If responsible persons had taken other rational decisions at the crucial time, Miss Ewing would never have been put in the situation of grave risk and perhaps Mr. Dixon would not have been at liberty to commit the crime."

At the subsequent trial, his barrister said, *"If responsible persons had taken other rational decisions at the crucial time, Miss Ewing would never have been put in the situation of grave risk and perhaps Mr. Dixon would not have been at liberty to commit the crime."*

Who, then, is the responsible person? Who should have made rational decisions at the crucial time? During our discussion of the Health and Safety laws and how they apply to lone workers in the next chapter, we will come back to explore this question.

First, in order to put this story in the correct context, we should acknowledge two things:

One: As we showed you above, statistically in the UK we lose one lone worker to a murder like this every year (1985-2008). It has been estimated that there are approximately 50,000 assaults on social workers every year.

(http://www.communitycare.co.uk/static-pages/articles/violence/).

Two: Considering the number of interactions between service users and their clients on a yearly basis—which must be in the millions—the risk of this happening to any one worker on any one visit is vanishingly small.

So there really is no need for thousands of lone workers to begin writing their resignation letters, for fear of being murdered! However, the risk is established and must be respected by workers and their managers. I think that this much is foreseeable: every now and then, a service user will try to seriously hurt or kill the community / social / health worker sent to work with them.

Perception and the Doorstep-Decision

One exercise which may be useful in relation to the story above is to ask ourselves this: "When approaching the front door of Ronald Dixon's house, knowing some of his background and history and recent state, what threshold of danger would YOU set for the meeting you are about to have?"

Low Risk? Medium Risk? High Risk?

With hindsight, it might be easy for us to say that the danger threshold for this meeting is Very High Risk—a danger level so high that it could pose a risk to life.

Now, what danger level do you think the woman who visited him on May 19th, 2006 had in her mind? We would, with all respect for her and the tragedy that was to follow, have to draw the conclusion that *her* danger threshold for this meeting was *not* set at *very high*.

Certainly, she did not set it at the level of "potential murder," because we know that she went into the flat with this man. As per the reason for her visit, she presented Dixon with the notification letter, which may have been the trigger for his aggression and which may have sparked the series of events that resulted in her murder. I think it is fair to say that she did not foresee any of these outcomes as she rang the doorbell and stepped into the house.

Setting your danger threshold

My basic danger threshold meter is a dial that I construct in my head. It is a standard pressure-gauge style instrument with a pointer in the middle. The pointer extends out to the edge of the dial, where at far left it may point into a large green zone, or at centre to an amber zone and then at far right into a red zone.

The colour codes are universally well understood:

Green: no foreseeable risk, no need to be especially attuned to risk, this is all under control. I am relaxed but aware of my surroundings, cycling through relaxed/alert attitudes.

Amber: foreseeable risk of danger, definite need to be switched on to signs of risk; this could get out of control at any moment. I am alert now and in a preventative attitude.

Red: danger imminent, exit this situation at first opportunity, situation is out of my control. I am now in a survival attitude and focussed on protecting myself.

If, through a lack of information, attention or experience, a worker's danger threshold is in the green zone and she is telling herself, "If this meeting goes badly, at worst I will get thrown out of the house," then the ingredients for a tragedy are already in place.

Many people have seen the often-quoted experiment carried out to demonstrate *inattentional blindness.*

(http://theinvisiblegorilla.com)

A huge percentage of the people in the experiment demonstrate this phenomenon of "not seeing what is in front of your face because you are concentrating on something else completely."

I don't want to spoil the surprising results of this experiment, so I won't describe it here, but please do go and have a look at the Invisible Gorilla. Incredibly, people don't see what is right in front of their eyes. They don't notice things. They have no recollection of certain things, cues or even people being in some circumstances. Why? Because they weren't looking for those things at the time. They were focussed on the task they had been given.

QUESTION: When you visit a client, are you in your "every-day" state, with no particular focus and simply "looking for the basketball," or are you in a more alert attitude and receiving signals, ready for when the man in the monkey suit makes his appearance?

Setting the danger threshold and being aware of the traps
Certain scripts—let's call them safety traps—seem popular when people at work discount their gut feelings about the danger they may be in. One of them is described above, and it is called the "What's the worst that can happen" safety trap. There are a few more common ones:

"It'll never happen to me."

After years of hard-won experience, it is possible that an experienced lone-worker's mindset could develop a script like this one: "I've done thousands of visits in my time, and no client has hurt me yet—those things don't happen to me in my work." Is it possible that these feelings of jaded denial could be blunting her awareness, or putting her permanently in a too-relaxed attitude?

"I'll get in trouble if I don't just get on with it."

Perhaps, through peer pressure and role-related pressure, a newer lone-worker could develop the following script: "My manager will give me a real earful if I go back to the office and tell her I decided to terminate this visit on a gut feeling." This discounts her professional knowledge, judgement and experience. It also points to issues about the adequacy of the supervision and support being offered to the worker.

"I can handle this; I'm up for the challenge."

Perhaps through some sense of pseudo-professional bravado and an emerging over-confidence, the worker develops a mind-set like this one: "I can handle whatever happens with this client because I know them, and anyway, if it all goes crazy today, it will make for a great story at the staff meeting next week." We then have a real problem on our hands—bravado erring on recklessness.

"This vulnerable person needs my /our help, and I am the person who can do it!"

I have started to call this the "Mother Teresa" syndrome—the widespread but dangerous thought that a social worker, community worker or healthcare professional has some special duty, over and above their legal duty of "reasonable care" to the vulnerable people they look after.

I often argue that when things turn bad for a lone worker in a house, such as being assaulted or locked in or kidnapped, how many vulnerable people are there now at that location? Two, of course! One who is vulnerable because of their complex needs, and the other because she is the victim of violence!

Don't be that person who discounts their own safety in favour of the other person's; instead, make sensible decisions about your safety (we call it making "reasonable decisions").

It is important that we recognise this "thresh holding" that happens on every doorstep. The critical moment is when the worker fails to adequately assess, "Considering what I know or don't know about this client, what is the worst that can happen?"

For all of these reasons, the mindset of the worker when setting that threshold of danger and the decision making which happen on the doorstep are all critical issues to lone worker safety.

The Role of Intuition in Doorstep Decisions

Gavin DeBecker, in his seminal work on personal safety, *The Gift of Fear*, offers us a crucial and often overlooked perspective on taking control of our safety.

His key point, illustrated again and again in his examples and case studies, is that when our innate survival system tries to warn us of danger, we must listen and take action.

He refers to this as the "gift of fear," and in more concrete terms offers a compelling explanation of how this intuition can be relied upon:

"Nature's greatest accomplishment, the human brain, is never more efficient or invested than when its host is at risk."

We are already experts at protecting ourselves (if only we would allow ourselves to be that expert).

Much scientific study is now being conducted into how the brain works, how our brain is wired for survival and the differences between emotional versus rational decision-making.

One example of this is in a book called *Blink*, by Malcolm Gladwell. In it Gladwell offers examples of "expert" decision making, which is based on just a small amount of information, called "thin-slicing." He asserts that an "expert" can make an accurate and dependable judgement of a situation within their expert domain, with just a few variables to work with.

This is a key point: "Experts who make snap judgments, based on very little information, are often accurate."

I believe you are an expert.

My training groups are often surprised and amused to hear that I regard many of them as "experts" at knocking on doors. Consider that, in an average working day, a home care worker visits up to 14 people. Many home care workers are experienced at working in the community for 8, 12 or 15 years, amassing a huge wealth of experience, involving thousands of hours of "practice" at:

- Noting the physical appearance of the outside of a flat or house.

- Quickly gathering information about their client's "state" when the door opens.

- Assessing hazards present in unfamiliar environments (their client's homes).

- Sensing changes in mood when interacting with their clients.

When we do this exercise, a home care worker with 15 years' experience typically has about 12,000-15,000 visits under their belt. Unfortunately, although it makes them feel experienced, it also makes them feel old!

Does this describe you? How many professional interactions have you had with your clients? Do the sums and see what you come up with!

When I call you an "expert," I really mean it! With thousands of hours of experience working with a wide variety of people in the community, it seems entirely reasonable to believe that workers like you are amassing what could be called "contact expertise."

So, when a door opens, somewhere out in the community and one of these lone workers experiences what DeBecker calls a "messenger of intuition—"

- Nagging feelings
- Persistent thoughts
- Humour
- Wonder
- Anxiety
- Curiosity
- Hunches
- Gut Feelings
- Doubt
- Hesitation
- Suspicion
- Apprehension

—then we must enable and allow these "experts" to make a sensible decision based on their experience, knowledge and professional judgement. Otherwise, if we are not going to trust their judgement, why would we allow them to work on their own?

We must also be cautious here. The very nature of intuition—its definition is "knowing something, without knowing why"—means that it arises as a feeling, a spark. Thus, intuition and insight often happens without a concrete, cognitive awareness of what the organism has become aware of and what caused it to fire off the important "pay attention" signal.

If in doubt, get out!

Workers and their managers should be mature enough, and have enough trust in each other, to be able to work within this domain where the tangible causes of concern may not be obvious. The alternative is to deny our intuition and insight, from which possibly the most subtle and eloquent risk assessments can be made.

"Insight is not a light bulb that goes off inside our heads. It is a flickering candle that can easily be snuffed out."

- Malcolm Gladwell

When the culture of a social or healthcare or community service values service-delivery over safety, then the trap is set for one of the tragedies we have noted above. Staff under pressure are at risk of trampling their intuition in the headlong rush to "get the job done."

This is especially so where they feel that their professional judgement and experience will not be respected.

We refer to Intuition and Instinct as the "Informal System" of detecting and avoiding danger. Along with informal buddy-systems (whereby colleagues on the same shift will check-in on one another throughout a working day) and informal information sharing in the staff canteen (where vital safety information is often a hot topic), listening and paying attention to intuitive feelings of danger is possibly the single most critical strategy that should be recognised and practiced within your team.

However, there are also "Formal Systems" of finding out about, assessing and then responding to potentially dangerous working conditions. In fact, there are legal obligations and duties associated with these "Formal Systems," and these will be examined in our next chapter.

Further reading for this chapter:

De Becker, G	*The Gift of Fear*	Bloomsbury, 1997
Braithwaite, R	*Managing Aggression*	Routledge, 2001
Maden, Tony MD MRCPsych	*Treating Violence*	Oxford University Press, 2007
Eagleman, D	*Incognito—The secret lives of our brain*	Canongate, 2011
Lehrer, J	*The Decisive Moment*	Canongate Books, 2009
Kahneman, D	*Thinking Fast and Slow*	Allen Lane Penguin, 2011
Klein, G	*Streetlights and Shadows: Searching for the Keys to Adaptive Decision Making*	MIT Press, 2009

Chapter 3:

Health & Safety and the Lone Worker

Employers have a legal duty under the Health and Safety at Work Act 1974 to ensure, so far as is reasonably practicable, the health, safety and welfare at work of their employees.

This act of parliament places a statutory duty on employers, besides their common law duty of care, to do "everything reasonable and practicable" to minimise the risk of harm which arise from hazards to health in their working environment.

Lord Skelmersdale even clarified how this applies to the risk of aggression and violence in the Social-Care workplace:

> *"Where violent incidents are foreseeable, employers have a duty under section 2 to identify the nature and extent of the risk and to devise measures which provide a safe workplace and a system of work"*
>
> -Lord Skelmersdale
> DHSS Advisory Committee on Violence to Staff

The Employer's Duty of Care

That Section 2 duty extends, in particular: "to the provision of such information, instruction, training and supervision as is necessary to ensure, so far as is reasonably practicable, the health and safety at work of his employees."

This implies that the employer must provide:

- information
- instruction
- training
- supervision

...sufficient to enable workers to complete their work in safety.

Information

Workers should be given information such as it pertains to their safety. For example, a client's history of violence or threatening behaviour towards workers assigned to them is a very good predictor of risk. Knowing this, it stands to reason that a worker who is tasked with delivering services to that client must be aware of the possibility of violence and aggression. This must be the case if they are to have the right level of awareness and take appropriate precautions in situations which might arouse the person's anger or frustration. This is particularly the case in, for example, learning disability settings where often the triggers for anger, fear, anxiety or frustration may be well known to the client's care team and fully documented in the client's care plans and risk assessments.

Instruction

Workers should be able to depend on clear and helpful instructions from managers about what circumstances might arise and how they are expected to deal with them in order to control risk of harm. A good example of a scenario where instructions will be very important might be those given to a worker who is doing an overnight shift in a house with a client with learning disabilities and a history of challenging behaviour. The particular behavioural cues, trigger phrases or actions, responses which defuse the situation, responses which worsen the situation and emergency tactics to stay safe (such as removing themselves to a room with a lockable door to isolate them from any physical violence) would all be important instructional points to be given to the lone worker going into that shift.

Training

Where a worker might be called upon to deal with an incident of aggression, they should be able to call upon training received which is sufficient and relevant in assisting them to try to safely manage that situation and their client. Likewise, if workers are likely to need to protect themselves physically, or to restrain their client by immobilising them to prevent harm, then it is self-evident that they should have had training in how to do so effectively and safely. Considering the risks inherent in physical intervention and restraint, including the risk that someone involved in the incident might be seriously injured or become a fatality, then the responsibilities of employers to provide training to workers who will foreseeably be facing physical challenges increases exponentially.

Supervision

Where a worker is on their own and dealing with the complex needs of a service user, then it seems common sense that they should be able to turn to a more experienced, knowledgeable or authoritative person for advice and guidance, and that advice and guidance would be available and useful to them.

Supervision means more than just a six-monthly meeting when both parties can fit it into their schedule. In health and safety law, supervision means that the person working in a risky environment knows that they have support and assistance within ready reach when they need it in order to stay safe.

"Reasonably Practicable"

When considering management of health and safety and all that I wrote above about employers' responsibilities, there must be a balance. Any risk must be balanced against the resources required, whether in time, money or effort needed to mitigate that risk or eliminate it. By pragmatically assessing the risk versus the resources required, the employer can decide what steps are reasonable to take to maintain a sensible balance.

The requirement for this balancing of risk and resource to be made implies the need for a formal, documented risk assessment to be carried out and evidenced, so that it can be clearly demonstrated that the risk was explored and the adequate control measures were put in place for it.

"Reasonably Practicable is a narrower term than physically possible and seems to me to imply that a computation must be made by the employer in which the quantum of risk is placed on one scale and the sacrifice involved in the measures necessary for averting the risk (whether in money, time or trouble) is placed in the other, and that, if it be shown that there is a gross disproportion between them—the risk being insignificant in relation to the sacrifice—the defendants discharge the onus on them. Moreover, this computation falls to be made by the employer at a point of time anterior to the accident."

-Lord Asquith Edwards v NCB [1949]

Let's look for a moment at a case where all of these issues appear to have come into play together:

The story of Lorraine in Wales

In 2011, a lone care worker in Wales was awarded an out-of-court settlement following a case which demonstrates why the Section 2 requirements are so important for managers to understand.

Lorraine was working in a learning-disability setting and carried out sleepover shifts in the client's own home. Lorraine was assigned a new client, but her employer failed to tell her about the new client's history of violence, which included assaults on 15 of her fellow workers when they had worked with the client.

At the time of the attacks, Lorraine and a male colleague were working in sheltered housing with the client, a woman, who had learning difficulties. Consistent with her history, the client attacked Lorraine one evening shortly after she arrived to start her first shift with her. Lorraine had not been trained in how to deal with violent or aggressive behaviour, nor had her colleague who was with her at the time. Lorraine was attacked from behind, but her colleague was unable to stop the beating because he hadn't been trained in effective restraint techniques.

When the support worker was finally able to free herself and call for help, her calls were ignored. Eventually, she spoke to her off-duty boss, who was able to get in touch with the on-call officer and area manager.

Rather than travelling to the house to provide assistance in person, the manager told the off-duty boss to contact Mrs. Morgan and tell her to lock herself in the staff room until the morning and to tell the male colleague to leave. She obeyed this request, staying in a locked room with no food, water, toilet or assistance for many hours, even as the service user was battering the door trying to get at her.

Mother-of-three, Lorraine, said, "The situation I was put in was unbelievable. I called for help and was ignored and then told to stay in a dangerous situation until morning. I felt abandoned and terrified in that room."

In the morning when Lorraine answered the door to her colleague, who was there to take over the shift, the client attacked her for a second time. Her colleague, again acting without any training, hesitated but eventually stepped in to assist her.

I invite you to examine this story and how it may demonstrate:

- A failure to provide necessary information about a serious or imminent danger.

- A failure to provide the kind of training reasonably practicable to deal with the likely risk.

- A failure to adequately supervise and instruct an employee who is at risk.

When reviewing this case with my trainees, I am often asked why Lorraine never called the police to help her. I can only speculate; however, I do wonder whether the "culture" of some social care work may have had an influence? How many social workers would feel they have failed their service users by losing control of a situation like this? Is there a type of bravado at work that would preclude calling the police to handle a situation? Or is there a pseudo-professionalism, or commercial reason for not taking the common-sense step of calling the police? Was Lorraine simply being obedient to her instructions when she did not call the police?

Nevertheless, Lorraine won her case. It would appear to be an easy one to prove—she was not given information which would have helped her prepare for or avoid the triggers which escalated this scenario. She had no training in dealing with the levels of violence that were a proven part of the client's behaviour. And finally, when faced with a crisis and calling for assistance, she was ignored at first, then finally given instruction which didn't reduce her level of risk; in fact, it merely prolonged it.

One also has to wonder in this situation, upon telling Lorraine that she should just lock herself in and wait until her shift had finished, what, exactly did the responsible manager do for the rest of her evening? Tuck her kids into bed? Enjoy a film on TV? Have a cocoa and forget all about it while her colleague was enduring this intense personal safety scenario somewhere nearby?

Clearly this is a case where Information, Instruction, Training and Supervision were not adequately provided to ensure the worker's health and safety at work. The employee took a case and won.

Assessing Risks and Training

Employers are compelled to consider the risks to their workers by the Management of Health and Safety Regulations 1999 (Section 3). The implied need for the assessment of risk and the putting in place of reasonably practicable control measures from the Health and Safety at Work Act 1974 was made more explicit and binding by the introduction of these regulations.

We have recently seen cases where the courts have clearly punished organisations for not providing the correct training or suitable and sufficient risk assessments in dangerous situations.

For example, in just one period in 2011/2012 the following cases were reported:

Dimensions UK was ordered to pay £44,000 in total when an investigation found that Dimensions did not have adequate processes in place to control the risk of workers being exposed to violence and aggression from a particular client. The client had kicked a member of staff in the eye during an incident in 2009. After the sentencing, HSE inspector Carol Forster said, "The risk of violence and aggression from clients with challenging behaviour is common in the social care sector. Workers can suffer not only physical injury but also psychological effects, such as stress and anxiety, which can also affect their family and social life." She added, **"Social care organisations have a duty to ensure that proper management systems are in place to control the risk of violence and aggression to the lowest level possible."**

A nurse was awarded £195,000 in compensation after being badly injured by a patient at North Tyneside Hospital. Staff in the unit had been asking for training in control and restraint methods for a period of seven years, but they had not been provided the training. The injury caused the worker pain and he needed surgical intervention, but he was left with limited movement in his arm. The worker's union brought a case against the hospital for negligence, and in 2008 a judge said that the hospital should have provided training in restraint interventions. The worker had to take early retirement due to his injury.

In the Ashleigh Ewing case, in which the vulnerable 22-year old was sent to deliver a letter to Ronald Dixon and was murdered by him, it was found that her employer had been placing **too much responsibility on frontline staff to carry out risk assessments**, and that even though tougher measures might not have prevented her death, they would certainly have reduced the risk. The HSE prosecuted her employer, Mental health Matters, for a breach of their duty of care. In 2010, the organisation was fined a total of £40,000 for that breach of their obligations to keep her safe.

Information Sharing
In 2012 we have seen how Information Sharing has become a key topic, with the case of Claire Selwood, a 37-year old mother of three who was working for Durham County Council as a Social Worker. Selwood was dealing with a case involving Graham Burton.

Burton had been staying at Cherry Knowle Hospital in Sunderland, where he was being treated for depression and post-traumatic stress disorder. Burton had told staff there that he was going to kill Claire Selwood "on the spot" the next time he saw her. He also told staff he had feelings of inner rage and admitted he had been violent towards others in the past.

After being released from hospital, he attacked her at a school one morning in 2006, stabbing her six times and leaving her bleeding almost to death. She suffered acute blood loss but recovered from her injuries.

An independent inquiry into the incident said that there was "a complete failure" by medical staff to warn Ms. Selwood of any danger. The Court of Appeal has accepted in 2012 that it is arguable that the NHS Trusts involved did owe her a duty of care and has allowed her to continue her lawsuit against her employer and the trusts. As a community, we await the results of this case with interest.

The Employee's Duties (that means You!)

Under section 7 of Health and Safety at Work Act 1974, employees are required to take reasonable care for themselves and the people around them who may be affected by the things they do, or the things they fail to do. The test of "reasonable care" is that the employee should do what a reasonable person would be expected to do in similar circumstances, with similar knowledge, training and experience.

This test of what the "reasonable person" would do in similar circumstances is one that is potentially confusing for some care staff. We often meet social care and healthcare staff who are under the impression that their job makes them somehow different, in the sense that because the people they look after are vulnerable by their nature, that the workers who work with them must take what we might call unreasonable risks in order to deliver services to them. This is the dangerous "Mother Teresa Syndrome" alluded to earlier, which places workers at risk due to their unreasonable expectations of themselves.

For example, we meet lone workers who are convinced that, if working alone with a vulnerable person in their home and faced with violent behaviour (such as with the Lorraine story above) then the care staff MUST stay and defuse the situation rather than leave the situation (and the aggressive person).

Somehow, they have become convinced that they would get in trouble for leaving the vulnerable person "on their own."

One common-sense response to this is to ask, "How many vulnerable people are there in this situation?" I want you to carefully consider our answer—there are at least two vulnerable people in that situation!

One, the vulnerable person who by their nature lacks emotional or cognitive capacity due to a learning disability, mental ill health, dementia or medical condition.

Two, the vulnerable person who is in close contact with an aggressive, potentially violent human being who wants to do them an injury during a rapidly unfolding confrontation for which they are barely prepared and trained for!

Again, we need to remember this: there are TWO vulnerable people in the situation, and now we are going to ask our employee to take "reasonable care" for themselves and others who may be affected by their actions.

Would it be reasonable for the worker to disengage from this aggressive situation? Could this involve leaving the room or house? If this left the service user by themselves, would this still be "reasonable"?

If instead in place of the violent, aggressive service user, there was a fire breaking out, which could expose our worker to risk of serious injury, what advice would be appropriate?

Why, we would certainly include the option to remove themselves from the burning building! In fact our procedures for dealing with fires is to compel the worker to leave the building!

Regulation 8 of the Health and Safety At Work Regulations 1999 has provision for circumstances of serious and imminent danger:

Section 8 Procedures for serious and imminent danger

8.   (1) Every employer shall -

(a) establish and where necessary give effect to appropriate procedures to be followed in the event of serious and imminent danger to persons at work in his undertaking;

(2) Without prejudice to the generality of paragraph (1) (a), the procedures referred to in that sub-paragraph shall:

(a) so far as is practicable, require any persons at work who are exposed to serious and imminent danger to be **informed of the nature of the hazard** and of the **steps taken or to be taken to protect them from it;**

(b) enable the persons concerned (if necessary by taking appropriate steps in the absence of guidance or instruction and in the light of their knowledge and the technical means at their disposal) to **stop work and immediately proceed to a place of safety** in the event of their being exposed to serious, imminent and unavoidable danger; and

- (c) save in exceptional cases for reasons duly substantiated (which cases and reasons shall be specified in those procedures), require the persons concerned to be **prevented from resuming work** in any situation where there is still a serious and imminent danger.

(3) A person shall be regarded as competent for the purposes of paragraph (1)(b) where he has sufficient training and experience or knowledge and other qualities to enable him properly to implement the evacuation procedures referred to in that sub-paragraph.

So, it seems clear that a lone social or health care worker who is faced with a serious and imminent and unavoidable danger (such as a service user who is combative) has the right to withdraw and disengage from that particular danger (Regulation 8(2) B) and should be prevented from returning to that workplace until the danger has been controlled or removed (Regulation 8 (2) C).

"But we have a Statutory Obligation to Deliver Services"

Greater Manchester, circa 2009

A district nurse is tasked with visiting a man in his flat to re-dress an amputation wound on his leg. He lives in a high-rise block of flats.

When the district nurse arrives, she is let into the flat by the next-door neighbour, who has a key to the front door. The man can't come to the door himself. She opens the front door and meets a strong smell of faeces and urine—the man's pet dog has not been outside the flat for more than a week and has been using the hallway carpet as a toilet.

The nurse picks her way between the faeces, down the hallway to the bedroom, where she can hear the man in his bedroom.

When she enters the bedroom, she sees that he is sitting upright in his bed, watching hardcore pornography on a large flat-screen TV. In his left hand is a remote control. She spots the dressing on his right leg, which she needs to work with, and moves around the bed to get access to it.

As she begins to re-dress the wound, the man begins to pause the video display at various points and ask the woman inappropriate questions about what is happening on the screen. She stays focussed, but becomes aware that the man is holding a large steak knife in his right hand, just a foot away from her.

She struggles to stay focussed but completes her task quickly and professionally. As she closes the door to the flat behind her, she feels all the energy go out of herself and begins to shudder as tears well up in her eyes and she begins to shake.

She is experiencing a sudden onset of the "parasympathetic backlash." Without realising it, she has just had a massive dose of adrenaline and the "chemical cocktail" of the survival stress response while she was in the flat. Her body, keenly aware that the danger has passed, now "crashes."

When she gets back to her office, still shaken by her experience, she tells her manager what happened and says, "I am not going back to that man's flat again. It's on my schedule for tomorrow, but I was so frightened and disturbed that I'm sorry, I cannot go back"

"Nurse," her manager responds in the immortal words known all over the country in meetings like this. "We have a statutory obligation to deliver services to these vulnerable people. I need you to get yourself together and go back to that client—I have no one else to do it."

In the above situation, if we apply the principles of Regulation 8, not only does the manger have the option to "allow" the worker to NOT go back to this situation of danger, the manager, in fact, has an OBLIGATION to PREVENT his staff from going back into a workplace in which there is still a danger which he has not yet taken steps to adequately control!

It may also be important to put the position of the "statutory responsibility to provide services" in its proper place. To our understanding, the hierarchy works like this:

- The Human Rights Act states that life must be safeguarded.

- The Corporate Manslaughter/Homicide Acts require organisations to protect life.

- The Health and Safety at Work Act requires employees to be protected from health & safety hazards.

- The Management of Health and Safety Regulations require that risks be controlled.

- Then, and only then, should the work in question (i.e. lone worker visits) be carried out.

The trump card—Human Rights
Article 2 of the Human Rights Act states that, "Everyone's right to life shall be protected by law." This means that the government, through any act of the state or a state body, must safeguard and protect life. It places a positive obligation on state bodies to control, through training and instruction and management, their activities in such a way as any risk to life is reduced entirely or minimised as far as is possible.

Every provision of every other act of parliament in the United Kingdom can be tested against the Human Rights Act, which therefore makes it the trump card in any discussion of statutory obligations and responsibilities.

Whenever a member of a government (or quasi-government) workforce puts a local authority or NHS trust lanyard around their neck and goes off to begin their work tasks for the day, they are covered by the first provision of the Human Rights Act—that their life will be safeguarded and protected.

When staff are completing tasks for their employer, they are at *work*, and therefore are covered by the ample provisions of the Health and Safety at Work Act and its associated Regulations.

There is virtually no set of circumstances under which another piece of statute law, regulation or guidance could supersede the requirements of the Health and Safety at Work statute law or the Human Rights Act Right to Life for a social or healthcare worker.

In simple terms, it may well be true that there are statutory obligations to provide services to vulnerable people in our society; however, those obligations are themselves subject to the rules about safety at work and the protection of human life.

No manager should be thinking about the importance of providing their service and prioritising their Key Performance Indicator targets in favour of their obligations to ensure that all of their staff go home safely to their families after their shifts.

Employment Rights and Refusing to undertake work

What if our district nurse from the above example decides that she cannot go back to visit that client with the penchant for porn and blades? What if she decides that her conscience, her fear and her responsibility to her family will not allow it? Can she refuse to return to a workplace where there is still a perceived danger to her?

EMPLOYMENT RIGHTS ACT 1996, Section 100

Health and Safety cases

(1)

An employee who is dismissed shall be regarded for the purposes of this Part as unfairly dismissed if the reason (or, if more than one, the principal reason) for the dismissal is that—

....

(d)

in circumstances of danger which the employee reasonably believed to be serious and imminent and which he could not reasonably have been expected to avert, he **left (or proposed to leave) or (while the danger persisted) refused to return to his place of work or any dangerous part of his place of work**...

It becomes clear that, yes, our worker has the right to refuse to carry out a work task if they believe that an imminent or serious danger persists in their workplace and it is not being adequately controlled.

I want you to focus on this information not so that you can note it down for use in a tribunal, after the stressful confrontation, violent assault or traumatic incident has occurred, but instead so that you can bear it in mind and use it to contribute to a sensible, mature and pragmatic conversation within your team whenever a discussion about safety and lone working arises.

A compensation payout or the momentary satisfaction from successful court proceedings against an employer for breach of duty of care can never truly make up for a lifelong physically debilitating injury, or a deep psychological trauma.

We advocate that workers and employers establish clear lines of communication whereby mature, adult decisions are made by professionals who trust their combined experience and judgement, who discuss issues of lone worker safety when they arise and who ultimately take responsibility for avoiding, as far as possible, the potential that any person on their team become a victim of violence.

Spend time on safety before it spends time on you

As a manager it may also be helpful to you, in order to justify spending the time on these issues, to note the following.

Health and Safety Offences Act 2008

The 2008 Act amends section 33 of the Health and Safety at Work Act 1974 and raises the maximum penalties available to the courts in respect of certain health and safety offences. It also makes imprisonment an option for more offences, and makes certain offences that are currently only triable in lower courts, triable in either the lower or the higher courts.

Section 37 of HSWA allows action to be taken against individual directors, managers and officers where a failure can be attributed to their neglect, consent or connivance.

Currently, individuals found to be in breach of sections 7 or 37 can face a fine not exceeding £5,000 on summary trial, or an unlimited fine on indictment. The 2008 Act, however, raises the maximum summary fine to £20,000 and introduces a term of 12 months imprisonment on summary trial, whilst a term of 2 years imprisonment and/or an unlimited fine will be available on indictment.

Corporate Homicide / Manslaughter Act 2007

The Corporate Manslaughter and Corporate Homicide Act 2007 is a landmark in law. For the first time, companies and organisations can be found guilty of corporate manslaughter as a result of serious management failures resulting in a gross breach of a duty of care.

The Sentencing Guidelines Council has suggested that the appropriate level of fine for corporate manslaughter will seldom be less than £500,000 and may be measured in millions of pounds. For health and safety offences that have led to a death, the appropriate fine will rarely be less than £100,000 and may be measured in hundreds of thousands of pounds or more

One lawyer commented that:

"The focus of the Corporate Manslaughter and Corporate Homicide Act 2007, and now this legislation (Health and Safety Offences Act 2008), is on the acts and omissions of the individual. This change of emphasis away from solely looking at corporate culpability to blaming the individual within the company is going to literally shock managers and directors who become subject to criminal investigations by the police service and the Health and Safety Executive. The Regulators will be seeking to flex their muscles.

If only for selfish reasons, those in charge of running the organisation ought really to be asking the question: "How sure am I that the company is being run safely?" And, "What's my role in

that respect?" For once, be that "doubting Thomas" and make sure that, so far as you can, the risk assessments, the safe working practices and the training are all in place and being followed. Do that and the emphasis of the new law will turn back to the liability of the company and not yourself."

– Poppy Williams, DLA Piper, www.info4security.com 3 Dec 2008

Further reading for this chapter:

Health and Safety Executive	"Five steps to risk assessment," INDG163	HSE
Health and Safety Executive	"Working alone: Health and safety guidance on the risks of lone working," (Leaflet INDG73)	HSE
Fox, B & Polkey, C & Boatman, P	*Managing Violence in the Workplace*	Tolley / Reed Elsevier, 2002
Paterson, B and Turnbull, J	*Aggression and Violence: Approaches to Effective Management*	Macmillan, 1999
Taylor, B	*Working with Aggression and Resistance in Social Work*	Learning Matters Ltd., 2011
Collins, S	*Health and Safety - Workbook for Social Care*	Jessica Kinglsey Publishers, 2009
Halstead, P	*Key Cases in Human Rights*	Hodder Education, 2009

Chapter 4:

Lone Worker Safety Devices

We met a training participant some years ago who described how she expected to use her personal safety alarm:

"Well, first, I would hopefully have it ready if I thought anything bad was going to happen. I mean, I am supposed to have it in my hand already and be ready to press the button. Actually, I think I need to pull a pin out of my device, to activate it. Anyway, hopefully, I would have it ready, and then if I could activate it; well, that's when the loud noise of the siren would hopefully distract the bad-guy long enough for me to get away from the dangerous situation."

The room went silent for a moment, and a lot of light bulbs went off over people's heads...crikey, our attendees thought, there's an awful lot of "hopefully" going on in that plan!

For years we have seen a lot of commercial innovation in building better personal alarms. We have seen the evolution from pressurised, gas-based personal alarms—just like mini-car-horns—all the way through to today's more technologically complex electronic sirens and the newer sophisticated communications technology and computerised tracking systems for lone workers.

"Everything works, in theory"

One of the key issues in terms of dealing with violence and aggression is what Lt. Col. Dave Grossman describes in his writings as the "universal human phobia" of intense interpersonal conflict. When faced with intense conflict and the threat of violence in our midst, the vast majority of us will experience phobic-level responses in our physiology and psychology. Books have been written on the emerging study of "combat physiology and psychology," which are starting to pick apart what happens inside the minds and bodies of people who experience sudden, explosive confrontations. These are the kinds of situations in which personal alarms and such devices are expected to be used, but how well are the devices being matched to how real people react?

The key questions may be:

- How easily can you access your personal safety device under high stress? And,

- When you have accessed the device, how easily can you activate it? And,

- When you have activated the device, what happens next?

How easily can you access your personal safety device?
Now, for the avoidance of doubt, I would like to clarify that our training team is positively inclined towards safety devices; however, their relevance and appropriateness in different circumstances needs to be contextualised and made clear to the people who are going to use them.

Accessing any type of safety device, whether a personal alarm, a mobile phone, a radio, a panic button or whatever, requires a number of elementary factors to be going in the operator's favour.

Alertness is one factor, embodied by the staff member, informed by the levels of information sharing and recording which is in place within their team, their organisation and their sector and their training in recognising any danger signs. As we have said, your intuition will tell you when you need to activate the device—in this sense it is still powered by a human being!

The next factors, *proximity* and *timing* are mainly influenced by the attacker; the ferocity and intensity of their actions will determine to a large extent the success of the actions of the device-activating person. Later on in this book I will explain a little about how we hope you can better manage proximity using some of our information about body language and "barrier signals."

Let's talk about timing and distance for a moment. In the most dangerous incidents, a highly aroused or motivated attacker can move with such quickness, ferocity and at such close proximity so as to render the worker's challenge in accessing a device very great indeed. Lone workers, especially the ones for whom the risks of physical violence are greater, typically work in close quarters with their service users—consider the size of an average living room, bedroom or hallway for a moment.

How quickly can an attacker cover the distance between them and the worker and deliver a blow? How much time might a worker need in order to recognise that they are under attack? How quickly then can they make the decision to activate their device and then finally execute the neural program for moving their hands towards the device to operate it? This *reaction time* issue is well studied in sports science, where performance under stress is so important. I believe these findings are underutilised in looking at how these safety devices are to be used in real, live situations.

There is some research we can examine to address this issue though—typically referred to as the "reactionary gap" theory and pioneered by police trainers in the USA. They asked the questions:

"How long does it take to react to a fast-moving threat?" And, "When is an attacker too close to allow an operator to reach for a safety device or weapon in time?"

Following experimentation, typically with live scenario-replication with role-players, a number of key outcomes consistently appeared. The one we want to draw your attention to in this context is that it is consistently found that a motivated attacker can cover a distance of 7 yards in 1.5 seconds.

That's right:

A motivated attacker can cover a distance of 7 yards in 1.5 seconds.

Acknowledging this standard, it is reasonable to ask what can our device-equipped lone worker be realistically expected to do in that space of time? Even considering the highly prepared worker, who has the device in their hand (rather than in their jacket or handbag) at the outset of the encounter with their client, what can be realistically achieved with a device in that tiny interval?

One of our training and consulting projects has been to work with client staff in the Financial Services sector, who told us many stories of their experiences with aggression and violence.

- One man routinely left his mobile phone in his car when visiting clients, before being locked in a house for an afternoon with an agitated client.

- One woman had had her phone swatted from her hand before being able to place her distress call.

- One man had been hit from behind with a baseball bat before he even knew his client was angry.

- One female lone worker, in a story we are aware of from 2001 (see below), was dead on her client's floor before her distraught husband began calling her phone in vain, looking for her.

Our key question about accessing your personal safety device is this: When you are in danger and need to deal with an imminent risk, what is happening while you are deciding to use, looking for, or reaching for your device? Our contention here is that while you are concentrating on the device, your attacker is still concentrating on you.

Mary Merry, 2001

Mary Merry lost her life one winter's night in 1999 when she was attacked by one of her customers as she collected debts at a notorious housing estate in Cambridge.

She had worked part-time as an "insurance collection agent" for Provident Personal Credit Ltd in Cambridge for three years.

Mrs. Merry made weekly calls on clients in their homes to collect repayments, and 37-year-old Robert Norton was one debtor over whom she had expressed grave concerns.

He paid her £12 a week to cover a £400 loan, but she often felt uncomfortable in his company and on at least half a dozen occasions had felt vulnerable enough to take her brother along for support. When Norton saw her brother, Michael James, accompanying her, he would not let the pair into the house.

Mrs. Merry had told her husband that Norton would sometimes lock her in his house or stand between her and the doorway.

On the fateful night, Norton, who had been sexually fantasising about Mrs. Merry, attacked her with two knives and a pair of scissors.

When she did not return from her rounds, her husband rang her mobile phone. Three times Norton answered it but did not say anything. When it rang a fourth time he destroyed it by stamping on it.

Norton admitted killing her but claimed manslaughter on the grounds of diminished responsibility, saying he had heard voices telling him to attack her.

- BBC News Saturday, 16 June, 2001. The Dangers of Working Alone

Great Safety Device—is it compatible with Human Behaviour?

Our human survival system is extraordinary. It works faster than the "plodding of logic" and can flood our body in an instant with a hormonal cocktail which enables us to achieve Olympian feats of strength, speed and endurance. Your deeply embedded DNA level survival system will always try to protect you in the face of sudden and aggressive threats in close proximity to your body.

The question is, how compatible are the actions needed to activate your personal safety device with the actions genetically wired into your body by millions of years of evolution?

Several works on the effects of arousal on behaviour, beginning with the Yerkes-Dodson analysis, help us to understand what happens in high-intensity, high-stress moments.

It is simplified here for brevity; however, when faced with an imminent threat, as a species we are wired-up to experience:

- A strong urge to turn our bodies and eyes to face the threat.

- Perceptual distortion (changes in time-sense, visual field and hearing).

- Difficulty in completing tasks requiring cognition (such as negotiating!).

- Intense physiological arousal (interpreted as: shakes, nausea, weakness).

...none of which are well suited to tasks such as:

- Staring directly at a number keypad (forcing attention away from the threat, contrary to what the survival system demands).

- Identifying individual numbers on a keypad (while suffering from 'tunnel vision').

- Using fine-motor control to push a button (while shaking or without fine motor control).

- Speaking calmly or slowly, remembering important facts like addresses or names or numbers.

It may even be useful to look at some of Lt. Col. Dave Grossman's writing on the subject of survival-level physiology and psychology in the critical moment:

"...an officer had to apply CPR on his infant daughter. He handed the phone to his wife and told her to dial 911, but she couldn't do it...she could not see the numbers and she could not use her fingers—even to save her own child's life."

In another story, when a woman found someone kicking down her kitchen door to get in her house, *"She fumbled desperately with the telephone but she could not see the numbers. She did manage to press the zero button, which ultimately saved their lives."*

Lt. Col Dave Grossman has stated in regard to tunnel vision that, *"The more stressed you become, the more narrow the tunnel. There will also be a loss of depth perception, meaning that the threat looks closer than it is, and a loss of near vision, meaning that you have trouble seeing close things. ... It is a terrible irony in some stressful situations, that at a time when you need your eyes the most, you may lose your near vision."*

Mumbo Jumbo Number 5

At one of our training sessions, the team had been provided with a system based on the use of regular mobile phones to make a "Condition Red" call to a dedicated Lone Worker Safety service. The system of work required the lone worker to push and hold the number "5" button on their mobile phone, which would call a pre-programmed speed-dial number and put them through to an operator at a call centre. This operator would immediately begin to record and monitor the worker's situation, with a view to bringing help to them if needed.

However, this particular system of work had serious shortcomings. First, the team had been informed by e-mail that they were responsible for setting up their own phones to call out on the number "5" speed-dial. Quite predictably, the staff team was not 100% compliant in achieving this set-up, which is the first point at which this expensive "system" was starting to fail and fall over.

The number "5" was chosen because, we have been told, every number "5" on every mobile phone keypad has a raised "dot" area on it which identifies it through touch as the number "5" button.

Sure enough, we find this to be true, even though the prominence and positioning of the 5 dot varies widely. In some cases it is off center, perhaps closer to the top of the button. When we say the top button, we mean when the phone is in an upright position, of course, not upside-down inside a pocket or handbag—and perhaps this all assumes you are not using a smartphone whose keypad is a flat touchscreen with a keypad lock on it.

Details, details!

A proposed experiment

What would we observe staff to do in a moment when they are exposed to highly aroused and aggressive individuals who are threatening physical violence to them?

We want them to find and press the number 5 button (and only that button, seeing as speed dialing any other number will not get the result they are looking for!). The worker may or may not be looking directly at the number and must achieve the task with fingers that are numb, shaking and desensitised by the action of cortisol and adrenaline in their bloodstream, causing vasoconstriction and robbing them of fine motor control.

They might have to look at the phone to find the numbers—if their vision allows them to do so.

All the while of course, the "bad-guy" role player will be applying pressure: aggressive posturing and threatening language, continually firing up the worker's innate survival system, which is located deep within their brain in the tiny and primitive amygdala fear centre.

The result is fairly predictable—system failure in most of the scenarios, with any variations in performance largely depending on the Awareness and Preparedness and Mindset of the workers.

The better prepared, more aware and more focussed the person on the task immediately to hand, and the lower the arousal level created within them by the scenario, the better they will perform.

There is a concept of "Stress Innoculation," which applies very often to staff in aggressive scenarios. Simply put, it says that the more experienced someone is in facing a particular type of stressor (such as aggression), the less impact their primal survival responses will have on their behaviour.

Of course, well-designed and implemented training can provide Stress Innoculation; however, in our experience across many sectors, the emphasis tends to be on "training the kit, not training the person." The result of "training the kit" is that even highly trained policemen will reach for their kit and put themselves at higher risk, rather than reaching out for the person who is presenting the risk in the first place and dealing directly with it.

In one video we show to our training groups, a policeman whose colleagues are being beaten severely by an offender decides to throw down his baton (which was the first device he decided to use) and instead use another device—CS Spray. He drops his baton and takes one... two... three... four...five...six seconds to find, unclip, draw, prepare and then deploy the spray on the offender. All the while the situation is still very much out of control, and his colleague is being punched and bounced off the furniture and walls of the room. Even then, the CS spray doesn't have the desired effect, because he is employing the wrong tool to the problem which is presenting itself to him.

In Defence of Technology

Our purpose in pointing out the deficiencies we see in the procurement and deployment of Lone Worker technology is not to decry their use, but instead to remind the social and health care sector that in the face of real aggression and violence, the person who ultimately holds the final power to influence the outcome of the interaction is the worker themselves.

By their behaviour, their body language, their positioning, their listening and questioning skills, their tactical awareness and their emotional commitment to safety, the worker alone will be able to exert the largest influence on what happens in the client's front room, hallway, bathroom or bedroom.

Nevertheless, managers have a responsibility to supervise their workers in such a way as to control the risks prevalent in their workplace. These devices do a tremendously helpful job of enabling this to happen in a relatively efficient and cost-effective way, answering questions such as:

- Does my staff have quick and direct access to help if they need it?

- Are the locations of my staff known if we need to find them?

- Have we demonstrably formalised our procedures for dealing with emergencies?

We are positively in favour of the new technology when:

- It is easy to understand and set-up.

- There are clear protocols about how it should be used.

- Its deployment comes with training in all aspects of lone worker safety.

- It is designed to work under the conditions of survival-stress.

- It is not a replacement for effective risk-assessment and safe systems of work.

Illustration:

Home Care Worker Killed

In 2007 in Hampshire, a 39-year old home care worker went to visit her client, a physically disabled woman who she helped with bathing tasks. Upon arriving at the home, the worker found a 47-year old man at the house. He claimed to be the boyfriend of her client, who would be staying there now.

The worker entered the house, unaware that the man had been convicted of violent sexual offences against women and was on the sex offenders register. Her client had already been murdered by this man eight days previously and her dead body was still in the house.

He attacked the worker, tied her up, interrogated her and took her cash card to withdraw £150 from a nearby cash point. He later returned to rape her and stab her twice in the neck, killing her.

The two women's bodies were discovered inside the client's ground floor flat after the care worker's husband raised the alarm when she failed to return home from work.

The murderer was convicted at Winchester Crown Court in 1995 of two counts of rape, and a further serious sexual offence, against a woman and was jailed for six years. Between February 2004 and 2007 he breached the sex offenders' register three times and was jailed on each occasion. At the time of the murders, he was being managed by police as a registered sex offender and was listed as "medium" risk.

QUESTIONS FOR DISCUSSION:

Can this kind of interaction—when a care worker meets an unknown person on the doorstep of a client's home—be risk-assessed?

Can a protocol be put in place for what the worker should do when unknown persons are in a property when the lone worker is visiting? Does your team have a clear protocol about "unknown persons" in your workplace?

Who, ideally, is immediately aware and alert to the fact that a lone worker has not finished their shift safely?

If lone workers in a team are regularly checked by phone call for location and safety during their shifts, perhaps even using a buddy-system, how would that change the dynamics of this kind of situation?

How would the provision and use of a Lone Worker Safety Device change the dynamics of a situation like this one?

Do you really need a device?
I want to make one final point about Lone Worker Safety Devices: they are an aid, a support system, a prosthetic for the ultimate safety device which everyone carries with them, their most important protection, safety and weapon—their brain!

Unfortunately, in our popular culture there are urban myths which seem to perpetuate themselves about what people should do to stay safe. One of these common gems of advice is that keys, combs, brushes or credit cards (yes, credit cards!) can be used as weapons in a Personal Safety crisis to fight off a mugger, rapist or other nasty person.

Now, I fully agree with the utility of some of these implements to become improvised weapons which can hurt Bad Guys. Certainly, if it is pointy, sharp, hard-edged or heavy, then it can be employed to good effect in a violent confrontation to help you. However, when an attendee reveals that she:

- Always holds keys in her hand like a set of claws, as she walks to her car

- Keeps a long sturdy comb in her jacket pocket and palms it when using elevators

- Always keeps a screech alarm in her handbag

... it invariably reveals an interesting dialogue for me.

I always ask, **"Why do you need it?"**

The answer is almost always that she needs it, "To defend myself with."

"What would you do with it?"

"I would scratch, poke, scrape, slam, stab, tear or batter the bad-guy with it!"

"What if you didn't have the comb, the keys or the brick in your handbag, would you try to defend yourself *then*?"

"[Light bulb]...Well, yes I suppose so."

"What would you use?"

"My bare hands."

"Would they be good enough?"

"They'd have to be, if I didn't have anything else!"

"So, do you really need these things—these improvised weapons?"

"No. I already have everything I need to protect myself; those things just make me more efficient."

"What is the real weapon system at work here then?"

"My own body, my own brain, my intent and my will to get home to my family."

When you step out of the shower in the morning, dripping wet, naked as the day you were born, are you able to protect yourself? Of course you are! Is it ideal? No, it is not ideal. But here is the certainty and resilience you must find for yourself: at any moment, you have available all the tools you need to protect yourself.

Still don't believe me? Here is just one example which illustrates the point!

January 24, 2008

A millionaire businessman single-handedly fought off three armed burglars—naked and without his glasses—after they put a knife to his teenage daughter's throat.

Bernard Dwyer, 51, who ran a construction business, said he believed they would all be killed and decided he "would rather die like a man than a dog" defending his family.

Despite being temporarily knocked unconscious and then stabbed three times in the head, he said he became "invigorated" by the sight of the attackers threatening his 13-year-old daughter, Aisling.

In a rage, he wrestled a gun from the arms of one attacker and then beat and chased the masked raiders from his home.

The Old Bailey heard how the armed trio turned up at Mr. Dwyer's luxury home in Uxbridge, west London, a day after battering to death restaurant owner, Helen Chung, 65.

Mr. Dwyer, who was born in the UK, but grew up in County Sligo, Ireland, was sleeping in his house with daughter, now 14, and son Danny, 20.

He said he ran out of his room naked and without his glasses after he heard an almighty crash and his daughter screaming.

He was confronted by the three men who ordered him to the floor at gun and knifepoint and demanded to know where he kept his safe.

But even though he was co-operative, the robbers, all wearing Balaclavas, beat him temporarily senseless with a knuckleduster.

Mr. Dwyer was knocked unconscious for a few minutes but claims he became "invigorated" when he came round and saw the third robber holding a knife to the throat of his daughter and threatened, "I am going to cut your f***ing daughter."

"I very quickly and very wisely assessed the situation," said Mr. Dwyer.

"These b**tards were out of control. We were going to die anyway, that's what I thought.

I thought if I am going to die then I would rather die like a man than a dog. The guy was standing over me with the gun and I thought if I can move the gun with my arm and make the bullet go into the wall I could come up and bash him."

Mr. Dwyer described how he pushed the weapon away from his face before rising up to strike his attacker. "I hit him several times; I hit him plenty," he said.

"The man with the knuckle-duster screamed, 'He's fighting back the b**tard, kill the b**tard, he's fighting back.'"

Mr. Dwyer, who was raised on a farm in Ireland, came to Britain with only £30 in his pocket and worked as a labourer but is now a successful businessman with contracts all over the world. He said, "Then the guy with the knife came over and plunges it in my head three times. The man with the gun ran off. I beat the man with the knuckle-duster out towards the door and closed the bedroom door on him."

But the businessman, who is married to wife, Jane, and has a second son, Shaun, 19, told the court how the pair would not leave and tried to push back into the bedroom.

"So we had another bout of fisticuffs," said Mr. Dwyer, "But this time I'm in charge of this battle. I let the door go and let them fall in and then, bam, had a go at them again.

"I have never used a weapon in my life and it was a great feeling. I grabbed the gun and bashed it across the knuckle-duster guy.

"Next thing is they took off and I chased them down the stairs. I bashed knuckle-duster man with the gun and I broke the handle on his head."

The burglars fled empty handed in the car they had stolen from Mrs. Chung minutes earlier, the jury has heard.

Mr. Dwyer was left with broken ribs in the attack as well as 30 cuts to his body and head including a gaping 3 cm wound in his thigh.

Dean Atkins, 26, and his brother Michael, 25, are accused of the attack on November 6, 2006. It is claimed the two also murdered Mrs. Chung the previous night after she refused to reveal the hiding place of her £218,000 life savings when they broke into her home.

Calling Out for Help? Beware Bystander Apathy!
Using a personal safety "screech"-type alarm might be useful as part of an overall escape strategy, but as discussed above it shouldn't be a psychological crutch.

What is the real utility of the siren on a screech alarm?

1) To tell people that you are in trouble and need help?

2) To cause the bad-guy pain from the high volume of the alarm?

3) To call attention to the event which is taking place?

4) To distract the bad-guy?

Screech alarms are my least-favourite personal safety risk-control measure, because of the following analysis.

Bystander apathy means that very frequently people hesitate and often fail to intervene at all. Even if other people hear a loud alarm sound, then there is no guarantee whatsoever that they will investigate the origin of the noise. Perhaps they will dismiss the sound as yet another car alarm being activated by a gust of wind.

If they DO investigate then there is absolutely **no** guarantee that they will then decide to get involved if they find a violent confrontation at the origin of the noise. Most people I have asked this question will tell me that they would certainly hesitate to intervene in anything that looked like a domestic dispute between a man and a woman, for example.

In Social Psychology this phenomenon is known as the "Genovese Effect," or more formally as Bystander Apathy. Sociologists have been studying the Bystander Effect for many years and it is named after a famous case in New York.

Kitty Genovese

On Friday 13 March in 1964, 28-year-old Catherine Genovese was arriving home in her built-up neighbourhood from a late night shift as a bar manager in Queens, New York. She was suddenly attacked with a knife by a man named Winston Moseley. She screamed aloud "Oh my God, I've been stabbed! Please help me!" Lots of people heard her—that's how we know what she screamed.

Moseley saw lights come on in nearby apartments. He knew people were watching, so he ran off, leaving Catherine to drag herself into a doorway. She lay there bleeding but still alive— she could have survived at this point.

Her attacker decided to return to finish off what he'd started because, as he later said in court, "It didn't seem like anyone was going to stop me!" Although badly weakened by now, she again screamed for help.

Of 38 witnesses who heard or saw some part of the attack (which took place over about half an hour in total), not one took action to help her. By the time the police were eventually called, she was dead.

Libraries full of research which has been undertaken into "bystander apathy" since this horrific crime has shown that the behaviour of the 38 witnesses is actually quite normal in the context in which they found themselves.

Loud Noises as a Painful Distraction

If you've read this far, then I hope you will agree with me when I make the following statement: if the bad-guy has gotten this far into a violent assault on you, then loud noises are unlikely to make him go away. If he is sufficiently aroused and adrenalised, then it is even possible that he won't really hear or register the screeching alarm. In any case, this is a less-optimal strategy—you need to be moving rather than clinging to a screeching alarm and hoping for the best. The best way to cause a painful distraction—if it really becomes necessary to do so—is to inflict one the old-fashioned way with your hands or other natural tool.

Calling Attention to the Incident

In all fairness to the screech alarm, calling people's attention is good, because with few exceptions outside of the scope of this book, there isn't a bad-guy you are likely to meet who wants other people watching, listening or intervening while he does his thing. He wants privacy, he wants to be away from prying eyes and he wants to have autonomy during the incident. As noted above though, this should not be the prime strategy— your bad guy may decide to abort his plan and run away if he thinks that there is too much attention coming his way. If not, you need a more robust plan. Fast-forward to our chapters on using Reasonable Force and on Behavioural Personal Safety to learn more about what may be next.

For now though, we want to focus on giving you a deeper understanding of aggression and fear and how they affect behaviour.

Further reading for this chapter:

Grossman, D	"On Combat - The Psychology and Physiology of Deadly Conflict in War and Peace"	PPCT Research Publications, 2004
Siddle, B	"Sharpening the Warrior's Edge"	PPCT Research Publications, 1995
Schmidt, R & Wrisberg, C	*Motor Learning And Performance*	Human Kinetics, 2008
Hancock, A and Szalma, J	*Performance Under Stress – Human Factors Series*	Ashgate, 2008
Klinger, D	*Into the Kill Zone*	Wiley, 2004

Chapter 5:

Understanding Aggression and Fear

"All Behaviour is Biology"

Your behaviour, who you are from moment to moment and how you respond to your environment is largely decided by which aspects of your primal self (the mainly survival-related behaviours bequeathed to you by your genetic heritage) are escaping the control and influence of your more sensible modern human brain—your higher-level consciousness.

There is a 1970's era theory of brain function from a scientist called MacLean which is a useful, although now regarded as over-simplistic, way for us to look at and understand aggression. The triune brain model can give us a very basic model or viewpoint for the biological roots of aggressive behaviour.

The Triune Brain

Brain Stem

The brain stem evolved some hundreds of millions of years ago, is the centre of the automatic, survival-focussed systems in our brains. In fact, it is sometimes referred to as the "reptilian" or "lizard-brain" because you have this, at least, in common with the pigeons on the street and the fish in the rivers.

The brain stem processes the most basic of survival challenges, the interface between the rapidly changing environment and the most fundamental things your body does to stay alive: the beating heart, the bellows action of your airways, the balancing of your physical frame.

Limbic System

Over millions of years of evolution and in response to the challenges of differing environments and circumstances, more specialised parts of the brain grew and developed to tackle unique issues: threat analysis, memory formation, data sharing, chemical synthesis in response to demand. The limbic system, encapsulating the brain stem, contains a collection of different brain structures which evolved to support and refine the basic survival system. The hippocampus, the thalamus and hypothalamus, the pituitary and the amygdala all operate on primal tasks designed to help you thrive. They process information and provide feedback using super-fast and comparatively powerful connections.

Neo-Cortex

The cortex is where higher-level awareness, consciousness and processing are carried out. This is evolution's most recent addition to the survival system; it is a sophisticated mass of connections, all working on a more long-term basis for not just survival, or thriving, but success. Your ability to innovate, to crunch numbers, to solve problems, to learn and create is all due to the wonder that is your cortex. Our ability to create sophisticated solutions to the challenges of our environment (rather than just running away from them or destroying them) is a result of what goes on in our cortex.

Joseph LeDoux's work on the *emotional brain* informs much of what we do in understanding behaviour and in designing and planning our training content and goes a little deeper on the emotional life of the brain. Let me now try to give you a basic primer on 'survival behaviour' from the point of view of what's happening in and to the brain.

The eternal conflict: impulse versus inhibition

We ask our groups: "When we've been out on the town for an evening, and had one too many glasses of tipple, what do we start to lose?"

In response to this, most groups know that the answer is not "our dignity!" as the old joke goes, but instead "our inhibitions."

Alcohol is just one of the ways in which the direction, focus and control which our higher self exhibits over our primal self can be weakened, allowing some of our primal behaviours out of the box. Just think of how hard it is to resist the kebab-shop or fish-n-chips on that walk home from the pub! Primal behaviour wins out over "sensible" when the conditions for weak inhibitions are ripe!

How powerfully our behaviour swings from one to the other depends on how we have been "wired up" by our genetic inheritance, our conditioning as we grew up and how we adapted our behaviour to our environment.

For example, it is well known that children who grow up in violent, unstable environments go on (often, but not always) to develop a greater impulsivity and a capacity for violence which is above that for children who have not grown up in violent, unstable environments.

Primal, survival-level behaviours that have been exercised time and again (such as with traumatised children, or soldiers in a war, or women in abusive relationships) can leave them with a well-exercised primal survival system which is comparatively "stronger" than the inhibitory systems attempting to keep them in check.

Success (or survival) in some environments favours impulsive and powerful reactions to situations which are perceived as threatening. Human beings have evolved a survival system which "hands off" to the primal brain in the presence of highly threatening, dangerous scenarios. This is known as the "Amygdala Hijack" when the primal brain lights up (comparatively speaking) while dimming or diminishing the influence of other parts of the brain on behaviour at that moment.

Can wolves climb trees?

Consider the scene, some millions of years ago when a group of our ancestors were standing in a forest clearing discussing the weather. Suddenly, a twig snaps, the humans turn and peer into the darkness of the thick forest and a wolf-pack breaks out of the tree-line, loping toward the group, low to the ground, predatory teeth flashing.

Our ancestors went "primal" and immediately took off, running, jumping and climbing their way through the forest bashing their way through the undergrowth in the opposite direction from the wolf's appearance, grunting with effort, and for all intents and purposes, looking very panicked. This is athleticism and physical endeavour at its pinnacle heart pounding, blood rushing, muscles bulging. Get away from those teeth!

Other humans present may have considered their options for a moment. Better to climb a tree or outrun the wolf? What speed can the wolf run? Is that faster or slower than a human can run? Can wolves climb trees?

What happened?

Well, in the end, the only question we need to answer is this: Which group was more likely to go home to make babies that evening?

Because you see, the ones who survived and made babies were our ancestors. The ones who spent those valuable split seconds engaging their cognitive resources, instead of their athletic ones, probably didn't make it!

Congratulations! You have been bequeathed the "dumb but alive" genetic inheritance. Your evolutionary heritage programs you to hit the GO button when you are threatened. You are not wired up for deliberation and negotiation when the wolf is bearing her teeth at you. Millions of years of evolution have been invested in this survival system and you got it for free.

Earthquakes, volcanos, tsunamis, avalanches, the actions of wolf packs and predators of all kinds, including other humans, have, for millions of years, selected the specific pattern of connections in your brain for optimal survival.

The Challenge of Face-to-Face Conflict Resolution

Unfortunately, this "dumb but alive" survival imperative, living deep within your brain's wiring, is (at least initially) completely at odds with the idea of resolving modern, complex interpersonal conflict peacefully.

Using clever (there is a hint—clever happens in the cortex) verbal strategies which induce voluntary compliance in your subjects does not come naturally to you. You have to understand it, learn it, practice it and expose yourself to this task in order for it to become a set of habitual behaviours. It must become habitual, because it is not natural.

Furthermore, consider that even if you are hugely experienced (and inoculated against the stress of interpersonal conflict) AND you are able to work through a conflict-resolution process in your mind, starting at the obvious points and working towards a negotiated solution, can your client do the same?

By definition, if you are in conflict with another human being, then THEIR survival system is also activated and is desperately trying to get them to focus their attention on running away from you or to physically beat you until you stop being a threat.

The survival physiology and psychology expressing itself in their system is primed to see you as an object to be avoided or silenced. Yes, one other thing you need to understand about the survival system is that it has a particularly negative personality. Like an angry bear, once awoken, it tends to see every next thing it must attend to as yet another thing to be biased against.

The illustration we use on our courses is about the person who wakes in the middle of the night to sounds of crashing and bashing in her kitchen. Edging down the hall to investigate the disturbance, she hears a door opening and more noises. Now, is she thinking, "Thank God, that's the police arriving!" or "Oh dear, now there's more of the burglars!"

Chances are she will interpret the new information as more bad news, and that is also true of the person opposite you in this confrontation you are having. Incoming information will be filtered through a negative bias.

Great place to be, huh! Your thinking brain is shutting down and theirs is only receiving negative messages anyway!

The Phases of the Aggression Curve
In order to know which strategies to use in the different phases of a confrontation, we have found that it is useful for workers to have a visual aid to mapping the process. The following analysis and tools are based on work by Kaplan and Wheeler who published their work entitled "Survival skills for working with potentially violent clients" in 1983. It remains today one of the most utilised models to represent the process of stress and aggression leading to a crisis.

I have asked hundreds of groups to look at this bare-bones graph over the years. I explain that the X-axis is a timeline with a beginning, a middle and an end, and that the Y-axis is an expression of the subject's level of stress or "arousal." I then ask my groups to tell us first what they think their subject would be feeling in each phase of the graph (1 to 7).

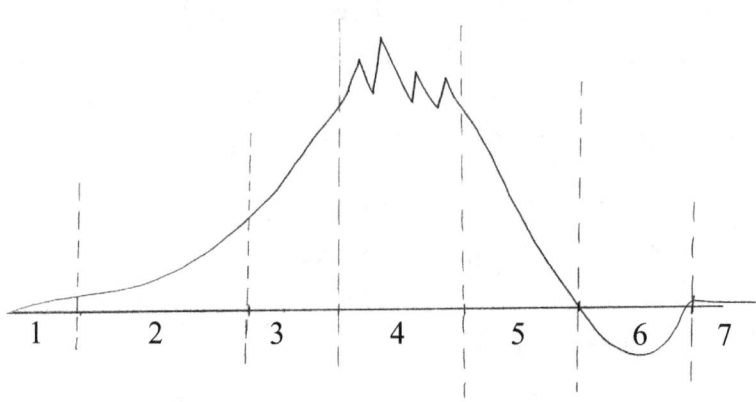

PHASE						
1	**2**	**3**	**4**	**5**	**6**	**7**
Feeling	**Feeling**	**Feeling**	**Feeling**	**Feeling**	**Feeling**	**Feeling**
Normal	Agitated	Aggressive	Out of Control	Relieved	Spent	Returning to Normal
Calm	Irritated		(Violent)	Calming Down	Tired	
Assured	Tense	Enraged				Recovering themselves
Okay	Uncertain	Confrontational	(Venting)	Reverting back	Upset	
Coping	Scared	"Losing Control"	(Acting out)		Remorseful	Normalising
	Worried		(Lashing out)	Regaining Control	Regretful	Coming to terms
	Anxious	Emotional	In Crisis		Depressed	
	Frustrated	Raging		Problem solved		Forgetting
	Angry	Panic				

The results of these informal surveys tell me that our groups of experienced Social and Healthcare workers, Housing and other Community-working teams believe their subjects feel the following:

PHASE 1: COPING

During phase 1, often referred to as the "baseline" phase, the person's behaviour is regarded as being "normal" or "calm." They are responding to the world around them from a point of relative calm and with little stress. They are operating at their normal level of arousal and are not experiencing any particular external challenge which is causing them to appraise the situation as threatening or negative.

I am always cautious to advise my training teams that this "baseline" is set at different levels for different individuals; for example, we all have friends who operate at a high level of excitement (the hyper ones), and friends who operate at a low level of excitement the majority of the time (the quiet ones). Understanding where this baseline is for a given client is then very important for us to monitor and gauge their level of arousal.

We also emphasize that the average person is never stress-free. Therefore, phase 1 does not describe a state in which there is NO stress, but instead a state in which the stressors that are present are not at a level which invoke a negative appraisal. In simple terms, the person is coping with the stressors that they are facing.

Coping is the ability to utilise resources that are at hand to deal with the demands of the environment you are in. Coping is being able to scratch the itch. Coping is being able to put on a jumper when the room feels cold. Coping is forgiving a minor irritation with a view to maintaining a long-term relationship.

In some sense, coping is about maintaining the long-term view about a short-term stressor and in this sense it is linked to impulse-mediation (suppressing primal reactions to stressors) and attention (directing the focus of one's thinking towards positive outcomes).

Having some tool in our personal-resources toolbox, which can be applied to the problem in front of us, is comforting and gives security. Reaching into this resources toolbox and finding nothing that can be usefully applied gives rise to feelings of threat, or stress. This moment, when external demands exceed internal resources, is the trigger-point.

PHASE 1: STAFF STRATEGIES

The key strategy to apply during the clients baseline phase is that of observation. Observation of the client leads to awareness of their state. Over time, it provides opportunities for learning about the client's habitual coping strategies. It is the bedrock of your practice as it leads you to the way in which you will talk, listen, comfort and reassure the person later on in the cycle. Observing the client allows you the realisation that they are no longer coping and have entered the Triggering phase. Professionally, this requires that the practitioner be "present" with the client and "mindful" of the client's state— professionalism issues which crop up again and again in busy health and social care services.

PHASE 2: TRIGGERING PHASE

The triggering phase describes the shift from coping to not coping.

Our survival system is triggered when the external environment (people, objects, situations, contexts, sensations) presents a problem to which we don't readily have an answer. The now-activated survival system is inherently negative in character and gives rise to feelings described above: irritation, frustration, anxiety, agitation, worry.

Here the minor stressor of the COPING phase becomes an irritation, a singular problem, identifiable because it is the one thing that demands attention.

To return to our itch analogy, when the itch is somewhere we can't scratch, then we are in the triggering phase. The itch demands to be scratched, and the demand creates urgency. Everything speeds up. We scramble for tools, desperately searching the toolbox for something, anything that will make the itch go away. A kind of panic sets in, an altered state of consciousness which focusses the mind on short-term goals. Short-term goals cry out for impulsive action and we rush for relief, often sacrificing long-term goals in the process.

The triggering phase inhabits the space between rational thought and primal reactiveness. Elements of both vie for a place on the main stage. Like the allegorical angel and devil on each shoulder, they compete for attention and often drive towards opposite fixes for the problem. The human and the chimp compete. The adult and the toddler struggle. The survival engine strains against the brakes of civilisation.

When the survival system is sufficiently stimulated, and the brakes fail to slow the system down, then the toddler wins, the chimp triumphs and human beings accelerate towards rage.

PHASE 2 STRATEGIES:
Phase 2 Strategies always have one commonality: they are "all about the client." The key strategy is to try to prevent the trigger from overwhelming the person. If their coping strategy for the stressor (or the trigger) is failing, then our objective early on in this process is to try to offer the person coping strategies which will work better. Often this involves some re-appraisal

of the circumstances, a re-framing of the scenario which makes it "look" not as bad or not as threatening.

Phase 2 strategies are all about the client:

"What do you want?"

"What do you need?"

"What can I do for you?"

"How can I help you?"

"You seem upset."

These questions characterise the core strategy used during phase 2—focus on the person and their needs.

PHASE 3: ESCALATING PHASE

The escalation phase emerges once the primal survival system achieves dominance, and the rationality of calm thought is drowned out by the louder voice of the fight or flight imperative.

The irritation, tension, frustration or anger experienced during the prior phase 2 now has a deeper quality in phase 3: the anger turns to aggression. The diffused feeling of unease about a situation turns to focussed attention on a specific cause.

One trainer I spoke with described this as the phase when the "Monkey" is in charge and the Monkey says, "FIX IT NOW! FIX IT NOW!"—a primal demand for instant relief. It also demonstrates the narrowing of attention down to one key demand. The client may even be repeating the demand over and over.

The descent from rationality to irrationality is observable. Each new stimulus experienced is perceived negatively, adding to the appraised level of danger and accelerating the increase in arousal. Focus and attention become narrower and narrower. A single issue dominates. A single goal becomes the objective. The organism increasingly grasps for quick fixes to this survival problem.

Senses are heightened; personal space, sounds, temperature, movement and so on attain perceptual primacy.

The acceleration during this phase is towards a state of rage—uncontrollable anger—a laser-beam of attention and energy, focussed on relief from the stress and provoking action.

PHASE 3 STRATEGIES:
In discussing this phase with a speech and language therapist some time ago, she advised me to seek out an old Larson cartoon that she called the "Blah, Blah, Ginger" cartoon. After reconsidering my high opinion of her and wondering if she had lost her mind, I did finally seek out the said cartoon and decided it made perfect sense!

The first picture shows a dog-owner berating his pooch: "That's it Ginger, this is the last straw! Keep out of the garbage cans Ginger, or else! I'm telling you this for the last time, Ginger, stay out of the rubbish—understand? "

The second picture shows the dog listening and is captioned "What the Dog Hears." "Blah, blah, blah, Ginger, blah blah! Blah, blah, BLAH, Ginger! Blah, blah, Ginger, blah?"

Dog owners in particular enjoy the revelation! In phase 3, the negative/primal state of mind reduces our cognitive ability to that possibly approaching that of Ginger. It is not really processing large chunks of information—it is just "gisting."

The gist here is:

Pointy finger + Red Face + Shouting + Rapid Pace + Angry Tone = **Bad news for me!**

With a client in Phase 3, your tone, pace, volume, facial expression and body posture convey much, much more meaning than the meaning of the words you use. The pace of conversation has more emotional effect than its content. Volume rises hand-in-hand with competition for dominance. Facial expressions and hand gestures become amplified.

We are biased in Phase 3 to paying attention to these non-verbal signals and to act on them; therefore, the strategy we should use to defuse the situation should reflect this.

Your key strategy in Phase 3 is to focus on "You"—your breathing, your body language, your expressions, your heart rate, your exit route proximity, your access to alarms, your tone, pace and volume as you continue to attempt the de-escalation. In this key way it is differentiated from Phase 2.

It is really important to understand this key difference: so many workers have related stories over the years about being deeply involved in what they thought was a negotiation/de-escalation script, when "out of nowhere," they got punched / slapped or shoved by their client. This demonstrates the value of knowing whether you are in Phase 2 or Phase 3!

If you were assaulted, ask yourself, "Was your client in Phase 3, but you didn't know it? Or did you change to accommodate it?"

PHASE 4: VIOLENCE PHASE

The next phase is when rage turns to violence. When aggression turns to action, when the door is slammed, the cup flung, or the punch thrown, then Phase 4 is in full swing (if you'll pardon the pun).

When we ask our groups what people feel during phase 4, it has always been interesting to observe the general consensus which tends to agree that there is almost no "feeling" or emotion which adequately captures what the person experiences.

Like Eskimos and snow, we tend to have many words to help us describe the emotions of Phase 2 (as described above), as we are so familiar with them, but the "feeling" associated with punching someone, or slamming a door, or throwing a cup, or kicking a television screen is a somewhat elusive feeling to describe.

One of our participants described this phase as "when you are so angry, you have that out-of-body experience." Indeed, many of our clients call this the "red-mist" moment, popularly understood to be a period of time during a violent episode when people "blank-out" for a few seconds while they are involved in a violent act.

This action, and the preceding rage, is almost totally the product of a critical stressor and a super-charged impulsiveness. Therefore, it is hard to pin an emotion to this; it is almost "pure" behaviour without cognitive input.

The possible exception to this is the sociopath, who may be able to access Phase 4 type behaviour while not having reached a level of uncontrolled rage or impulsiveness. For a true sociopath, a true bad-guy, it may be possible for them to be punching you in the head while wondering where they are going to buy dinner with your money later that day.

PHASE 4 STRATEGIES:
You have two choices in Phase 4—engage or disengage. For most lone workers, you will be disengaging, which means exiting the room, building or situation in which you are working. As discussed, the various pieces of legislation and regulation support you making this decision and making yourself safe in this way.

Unfortunately, due to the nature of aggression and especially with violent assaults, you may need to use force to enable your disengagement from a situation. If the violent person has attached themselves to you, then you may have to remove their hold on you. If the violent person is a motivated and committed attacker, then you may have to physically engage with them in order to win time for you to reach a door and exit the situation. If the violent person has somehow trapped you (by locking a door, or barring your exit) then you may not have the simple and direct option of walking through a doorway.

In many of these cases, you may have to consider the use of physical force to make it possible for you to escape and exit the situation.

The key strategy in Phase 4: Protect yourself (Be Home Safe)

PHASE 5: RESOLUTION PHASE

Once the action phase has had its effect—a short-term release of high-level tension directed at the cause of the stress—then the problem has been solved. The threatening situation has found a resolution. Unfortunately, in this model, arriving at the resolution phase, having passed through phase 4, means that someone got hurt, something got broken or otherwise there was a complete loss of self-control, each of which has consequences.

The resolution phase is marked by feelings of relief and release (that feeling of having scratched the itch).

PHASE 5: STRATEGIES:

Remember, from our earlier chapter on Health & Safety risk management, you are allowed to proceed to a place of safety in the absence of instruction and in the light of your own knowledge and ability if faced with some serious or immediate danger which you cannot avoid. Furthermore, your manager/supervisor should prevent you from returning to an unsafe workplace.

Truth be told, you as a lone worker shouldn't be "there" for Phase 5, because if you got to Phase 4, then you are not available to the client any longer. We typically see workers in residential care settings needing to think about Phase 5 strategies, but not workers who visit people in their own homes to carry out services. As a lone worker your Phase 4 strategy to cope with their total loss of control and their violent behaviour is to make yourself safe and leave the situation. You should not be present for phase 5.

For what it is worth, Phase 5 strategies look a lot like Phase 2 strategies with a focus on the person's feelings, needs and mitigating, reducing or removing any remaining triggers. Consider that, when the "chimpanzee" who took over the autopilot in phase 3 has dealt with the situation and prevailed over the survival threat, it will be time then for the "human" part of the brain to regain its rightful place in directing things.

Reassurance may be a particularly strong tactic for phase 5, as the person, with an increasing (returning) level of self-awareness, may feel disoriented, shocked, surprised or disappointed about their loss of control during phase 4. In some way, your task here is to convince the "chimp" that they can go back to dreaming about peeling bananas, in the background, dormant with the threat now receded.

Remember though the words of Mr. Miyagi: "best defence, no be there!"

PHASE 6: POST CRISIS PHASE

After the sudden build up and release of energy during phases 2-4, the body often then requires a period of physiological recovery (called the "parasympathetic backlash"). Tiredness, extremes of emotion and perhaps depressed feelings characterise this phase.

Often there is a reflection and a realisation of the wider consequences of the Phase 3 & 4 behaviour. Remorse, regret and guilt are also possible resultant feelings here - representing a very human response to the aftermath of a crisis.

It is as if, having been quite absent during the super-primal moment in phase 4, the "human" brain now returns and desperately tries to make sense of what happened in the period in which it was not running the show. Deep introspection, self-analysis and assessment may follow and powerful realisations may happen.

PHASE 6: STRATEGIES:

The same arguments about "not being there" apply to Phase 6. Unless there has been a management intervention and reassessment of risk, then you are unlikely to be present with your client while they go through Phase 6—their "down" time after a violent episode.

If you do see the client during this time, then your aim will be on preventing future incidences of the kind of behaviour you saw in Phases 3 and 4. You may focus on what they were feeling during Phase 2 and then you might also introduce a discussion about immediate consequences for them, their service package, the staff involved and so on. You might try to work out preventive measures—new coping strategies—for the "next time" too.

PHASE 7: RECOVERY PHASE

This phase is characterised by a return to more baseline behaviours and arousal levels, a recovery from the process of escalation and de-escalation. They recover themselves, back from the crisis and their feelings in the aftermath.

PHASE 7: STRATEGIES:

At this point we would like to think that you are back at the office, writing up your incident report, discussing what happened with your manager and preparing an update to the risk assessment and plan for this client, or this type of behaviour.

In an earlier chapter, we stressed the importance of information recording, reporting and sharing and that it is so critical to the overall safety of your sector. The more information we have about what is going on, and the more key people that have access to this information, the better the predications everyone can make about how safe it is to work with your clients. Don't neglect this essential piece of the process!

Further reading for this chapter:

Morris, D	*The Human Zoo*	Vintage, 1994
Morris, D	*The Naked Ape*	Corgi Books, 1967
Morris, D	*Manwatching - A Field guide to Human Behaviour*	Grafton Books, 1977
Winston, R	*Human Instinct - How our primeval impulses shape our modern lives*	Bantam Books, 2002
Goleman, D	*Emotional Intelligence: Why it can matter more than IQ*	Bloomsbury, 1996
Thompson, G & Jenkins, J	*Verbal Judo - The Gentle Art of Persuasion*	Quill, 1993
Fisher, R & Ury, W	*Getting to Yes - Negotiating an Agreement Without Giving In*	Random House, 1981

Chapter 6:

Understanding Conflict Triggers and Tactics

What is going on in Phase 2, the triggering phase? Having surveyed hundreds of social care and healthcare professionals over the years, I believe that we have arrived at a succinct list of the reasons why service users become upset, angry, frustrated and aggressive towards workers.

In trying to distill the causes of frustration down to the most succinct forms possible, I have tried to create basic statements of need. The following five statements seem to sum up the vast majority of "challenging behaviour" faced by lone workers in health and social care that I have met.

The 5 Essential Flashpoint Statements:

Don't embarrass me!

Don't change things!

Give me control!

I'm not comfortable with you!

Don't treat me differently!

Needs and Behaviour

In social science, the work of Abraham Maslow in delineating the fundamental needs which drive human behaviour is well known. His "Hierarchy of Needs" as it is known, has a central place in many social theories which describe people's behaviour.

Simply, it states that the most absolute and fundamental needs of a person are air, food, water, sleep, excretion and so on—basic physiology. Basic "conflict management" theory states that if I somehow threaten your access to air, food, water, sleep or another of these, then the path to aggression and violence will be swift and powerful. Just imagine how long it might take you to take aggressive action if I stopped the supply of air to your lungs by grabbing your throat. This goes a long way toward illustrating the importance of that particular need. Similarly, we have seen legal/philosophical arguments about the justification a starving person may have for killing someone who is withholding food from them. Fundamental needs have a way of evoking primal behaviours.

Maslow then described a series of layers built upon this base layer of physiological needs, which were ordered in decreasing urgency. Next on the list came securing shelter, resources, protecting the family, investing in personal health, enhancing dwellings, and so on. Many of these still relate to survival but have a longer-term focus (perhaps "thrival" is more apt).

In the middle of Maslow's hierarchy are the social needs: friendships, family bonds, professional teams, intimacy and the feelings these relationships give us—self-esteem, confidence, achievement, respect and support.

Finally, at the top of his hierarchy, Maslow placed a group of needs related to self-actualisation, the realisation of individual internal drives towards feelings of success and accomplishment. Meeting this level of need is like fulfilling a calling or achieving a burning ambition. For better or worse, it is the reason we have the X-Factor on television!

A challenge to Maslow's neat hierarchy though, is a comparatively recent collation of brain research carried out by David Rock of the Neuro-leadership movement, which was founded on the belief that organisations should use the evidence base from neuro-science and psychology as the guiding principles in the influence of people's behaviour and performance.

David Rock, combining the results of many studies and psychological research, found that in fact, Maslow may have been too quick to relegate the social aspects of human need. Rock suggests that, having literally seen the brain at work in social experiments (through the use of FMRI imaging and suchlike), in fact, our brains register some social threats as keenly as they register physical threats.

He cites examples of people being put in situations where their relationships with the people around them are threatened in some way and how their brain appears to activate in the same way as when a person is caused pain by a pinprick.

Physical pain evokes the same brain activity as social pain
In an effort to distill these ideas, Rock created the SCARF model to explain how the social brain monitors the environment for potential threats (and rewards).

How the Social Brain influences behaviour

- **Status**
- **Certainty**
- **Autonomy**
- **Relatedness**
- **Fairness**

1: Status—"Don't embarrass me!"

The relative social, professional, or other standing of someone.

People pay a lot of attention to protecting and building their status in the "pecking order." People have an innate sense of where they are on this pecking order (their sense of self-esteem) and where they perceive you to be on it (their sense of authority).

Status Rule of Thumb:
If I threaten someone's sense of status / importance / esteem, they respond negatively. If I enhance someone's sense of status, they respond positively.

There is a threat to a person's sense of Status when they hear:
You are inept / incapable / incompetent.

I don't respect you / I am better than you.

You are not as (insert adjective) as I thought you were / as you used to (or should) be.

You know they are experiencing a Status Threat when they communicate:

Do you know who I am?

Don't embarrass me!

Who do you think you are?

I can do this by myself!

How dare you do that / say that / imply that to ME!

Offer Status enhancers:

Listening carefully and respecting their point of view.

Acknowledgement of the person's value or importance (showing respect).

Positive comparisons.

Genuine compliments about achievement or effort.

2: Certainty—"Don't change things!"

Prediction is the primary function of the brain—it likes to be sure of itself. Imagine that moment when you arrive at the airport to go on holidays and look up at the departures screen: "FLIGHT DELAYED." Everything has been planned, you are two hours early for the flight, the transfer at the other end is scheduled, and the hotel booking is made. You can SEE yourself sitting poolside sipping a delicious cocktail in just a few hours—and what just happened? Your carefully constructed day, your predicted outcome from your effort, is now a crumpled mess, thrown in a vortex of change and uncertainty.

Delayed until when? Will the flight be cancelled? Will the transfer taxi wait? Will the hotel re-allocate the room? Will the bar close before I can order my cocktail? Has this airport screen been updated with the latest information? All is now uncertain, and depending on how you are wired-up for "certainty," your brain hates this.

Some of us work better with uncertainty than others. In general though, lots of our brain activity is dedicated to predicting what's going to happen next. It is a major reason for success and survival—the ability to predict a variety of likely outcomes and plan for them. Where we get tripped-up is when the outcome matches none of our predictions. This registers as a potentially threatening situation, and our brain responds with stress hormones, preparing for the worst.

Certainty Rule of Thumb:
If I threaten someone's sense of certainty / stability / sureness then they will respond negatively. If I can enhance their sense of certainty they will respond positively.

People experience a Certainty threat when they hear:
I'm your new / replacement (significant decision-making person in their life).

Everything's changed now; there is a new system for that.

FWIW U may hav no IDA what this complicated J4RG0N means.

You know they are experiencing a Certainty Threat when they say:
What's going on?

Don't change things!

Who are you? Where is my usual person?

This is different to before / to what I expected / to what I was told

I'm confused...

Slow down!

Offer Certainty enhancers:
Go Slow!

Offer clarity; explain things clearly.

Ask questions to elicit more clarity about the situation they are in ("stabilise" things).

Establish rules early and be consistent with them.

Proactively assist the prediction process ("This is what's going to happen next.").

3: Autonomy—"Give me control!"
"freedom from external control or influence"
"independence" "freedom" "self-determination"

The perception of being in control is a major driver of behaviour. In order to survive and thrive, the ability to choose action from a broad list of alternatives (autonomy), rather than being confined to minimal options, is more optimal for survival, considering just how random the world can be!

This domain is linked to Certainty, as the reliability of the prediction is used to then make decisions about what course of action the person can take.

In the UK, a popular comedy character is a worker who must consult her computer system whenever someone asks her a question. Invariably, the computer's answer is "No" and so was born the catchphrase "Computers says NO!" It doesn't matter the question, the computer—this inanimate, cold, non-communicative, un-swayable machine—could decide an issue definitively and without recourse.

The response from the questioner to the "Computer says NO!" response is, of course, dismay, frustration and anger. When there is no control, no hope for control, no avenue for alternative options or compromise, then we have the proverbial "Hobson's Choice" (take it or leave it). When there is no choice, there is no Autonomy.

Even a Dilemma (a choice between two or more options, none of which is attractive) is better than no choice at all, as at least it offers the perception of choice. Identifying a False Dilemma (where only two choices are considered, when in fact there are others) is in fact a great way to offer a person autonomy, as you can then encourage them to take control by thinking of new ways to tackle a problem.

We often stress that a person who is deprived of options, alternatives and control can be one of the most dangerous people to work with. The final option is to resort to violence, either to others or to themselves, often with tragic consequences.

Autonomy Rule of Thumb
If I threaten someone's sense of control / choice / agency they will respond negatively. If I can enhance their set of options, give them more control or choice, they will respond positively.

People experience an Autonomy Threat when they hear:
This is mandatory.

You have to do this or else (negative outcome).

It's my way or the highway.

The schedule says now or not at all.

You know they are experiencing an Autonomy Threat when they say:
I don't want to!

You can't make me!

Isn't there any other way?

Must we do it this way?

I've got no other option?

Offer Autonomy enhancers:

— Offer them choice and control, or the perception of these.
— Re-appraise the situation and search for alternatives.
— Ask for the person's own best next option.

4: Relatedness—"I'm not comfortable with you!"
"belonging to the same family, group, or type"
"connected" "linked" "kindred" "akin" "comparable"

The safety domain is an interesting and powerful one. Imagine that your brain operates a friend-or-foe scale, and that throughout each day a part of your brain appraises every person you meet and then places your relationship with that person on that scale somewhere between enemy and friend, between opponent and ally. It is apparent that people are classed as friend or foe—and quickly.

Commonalities are what the brain seeks. People with similar life circumstances, similar job types, similar family situations, similar fashion sense, similar upbringings—these all feed the process of establishing the friend-or-foe rating of the people you meet.

With strangers, you may not know anything about the person, and therefore you go by what you do know, what you can perceive about them, your first-impression—gender, age, size, skin colour, accent, tone and pace of their speech.

All of these signals will contribute to a lightning-fast analysis of whether or not you feel "safe" with this person. And this "safeness" is measured in terms of how well you can empathise with one another, how well you can (or are likely to) understand one another's needs. The essential question is about how "safe" you feel in that person's presence.

Now consider the care worker who arrives on a doorstep for the first time. She is 22 years old and is from London, went to University and is very informal in her interpersonal approach. She is going there to work with an 80-year old man, who is from Inverness, who worked on a private estate as a gamekeeper his whole life and appreciates formality in all his dealings.

How comfortable will they be together on first meeting? The essential question about Relatedness is: How much energy will they need to invest in the relationship in order to reach a level of comfort with one another? Work will need to be done to move the "other" person from the stranger area of the scale to the friend area of the scale. This is perfectly natural; it just needs to be acknowledged that this requires energy and attention.

Relatedness Rule of Thumb

Threaten someone's sense of relatedness by appearing to be a stranger or an opponent and they will respond negatively. Enhance their sense of safety and comfort with you by establishing two-way empathy and they will respond positively.

People experience a Relatedness Threat when they sense:

You have no reference point to understand their needs.

They have no way to relate to who you are / where you come from / what drives you.

There is nothing in common between you and them.

You know they are experiencing a Relatedness Threat when they say:

Where is my usual person?

You wouldn't understand this anyway.

Where is your accent from?

Not with strangers around!

Offer Relatedness enhancers:

Be at ease; remember, you are trying to establish a feeling of safety between the two of you.

Find commonalities (family, sports, hometown, and interests).

Offer the other person interesting (appropriate) information about yourself.

5: Fairness—"Don't treat me differently!"

"In accordance with the rules or standards"
"Just or appropriate in the circumstances"

"equitable" "even-handed" "non-partisan" "tolerable" "decent"

Reciprocity is a bedrock of the deeper-level behavioural interactions we have with others. It is the basis of trade and politics and is defined in many different spheres of human activity—the in-kind response to the behaviour of others. When we give, we expect to receive equitably, and in fact, the principle works in the alternate direction also: when we receive, we expect to give.

So, when two people interact on any level, there is often an unspoken expectation that the relationship should be an equitable one that both parties should benefit equally in some way or another from the interaction.

This also applies to compliance with rules. If I am to be restricted somehow by an established set of rules, then I will expect that others will similarly be restricted and not somehow given an advantage over me. Consistency of the equitable relationship is key; we all have a very keen sense of any application of the Double Standard (where there is an unjust application of different sets of principles for similar situations).

Fairness Rule of Thumb
Threaten someone's sense of fairness or reciprocity and they will respond negatively. Enhance their sense of getting a fair deal, striking a bargain or an equitable return, and they will respond positively.

People experience a Fairness Threat when they sense:
You are treating them differently to someone else.

They are not getting what they think they are entitled to.

They gave you something and aren't getting back.

You know they are experiencing a Fairness Threat when they say:
Give me a break!

(Someone else) got (something) from your organisation, why not me?

This just isn't fair!

But I did everything you asked and now you're saying I can't...

We arranged a 10 am appointment and you missed it!

Offer Fairness enhancers:
— Introduce some give and take.

— Offer them something (I can do this thing for you...).

— Re-appraise the balance of inputs between you and the other person (is it really unfair?).

Further reading for this chapter:

Rock, D	*Your Brain at Work*	Harper Business, 2009
Rock, D	"SCARF: a brain-based model for collaborating with and influencing others"	www.neuroleadership.org, 2008
LeDoux, J	*The Emotional Brain*	Phoenix, 1998
Ekman, P	*Emotions Revealed - Understanding Faces and Feelings*	Phoenix, 2003

Thompson, G & Jenkins, J	*Verbal Judo - The Gentle Art of Persuasion*	Quill, 1993
Fisher, R & Ury, W	*Getting to Yes - Negotiating an Agreement Without Giving In*	Random House, 1981

Chapter 7:

Receiving and Broadcasting Body Language Signals

Recognising signs of aggression in the other person's body language

As discussed above, interpersonal conflict will induce a release of adrenaline in the person's body and cause a number of changes in their physiology. Some of these physiological changes will have outward, observable results. For example:

- Facial colour change
- Change in breathing
- Movements become larger and "jerky"
- Pacing and Repetitive movements
- Suddenly speechless or monosyllabic
- Staring or "looking through you"
- Aggressive Gestures

Facial colour change

The drastic changes in heart rate and blood pressure cause a change in blood-flow to the extremities. Interestingly, for anger, we usually register the "red-face," but for fear we register the "whitening" of the face. Our suggestion is that either condition should warn you of a deep and significant adrenaline rush in the person's body which is making them more dangerous/less rational, and therefore you need to pay heed. This is a good time for you to take a step back and introduce a "barrier signal."

You will observe: reddening or whitening of the face

Change in breathing

In order to feed the engine of survival athleticism, the body initiates a process of "vasoconstriction," essentially squeezing the blood vessels of the extremities tight and thereby forcing the blood volume to concentrate in the torso. This has the effect of making the significant proportion of a person's blood volume to be rushing around near their heart and lungs. The engine driving athletic performance is at once delivered large volumes of vital oxygenated blood which will drive its activity. The body also increases the rate at which it is sucking air in and pushing it out of the body, thus allowing a more rapid rate of gas exchange and therefore, in simple language, putting more coal in the furnace.

You will observe: deepening (heaving) and/or quickening of the breathing, a deep inhalation or exhalation

Movements become larger: "jerky"

Our survival system is wired for sprinting / climbing / jumping out of the way of dangerous scenarios. It has not yet wired itself to "maintain an aura of dignity" or "show a calm and mature manner" when escaping from serious threats. Therefore, the evolutionary imperative has become "use the big push/pull muscles of the chest and the powerful thrusting muscles of the legs to get away from danger." In summary, the larger muscles (which contribute most to "gross motor movement") are engaged while the smaller muscles (which contribute to fine or complex motor movement) are disengaged, leaving us with the very expressive, demonstrative behaviours that we all recognise as what Rory Miller has termed the "Monkey Dance" in his books (for example: *Meditations on Violence*).

You will observe: expressive, wide, large-format movement with powerful, tense qualities.

Pacing or Repetitive movements
In an effort to "work off" some of the excess energy now coursing through the system, the person (possibly quite unknown to themselves) will initiate some repetitive movement cycle or pattern. The most commonly known one of these is pacing. The person will, quite without conscious volition, start to walk up and down in order to dissipate the tremendous energy building up (without sufficient outlet) in their legs. Their legs want to carry them far, far away from this stressful situation—or power them to climb a tree, or kick something really hard.

Sometimes, the pattern is not pacing, but instead some kind of repetitive movement, such as stroking their arm, or nodding, or shaking their head. It might be a self-comfort signal.

Something about our crisis, survival behaviour favours repetition (or perseveration of an action once it has begun). Notice this pattern and take a step to acknowledge it.

You will observe: a repetitive pattern, most often pacing, but also possibly any other repeated action.

Suddenly speechless or Monosyllabic

The same issues effecting people's fingers (vasoconstriction and loss of sensation) will affect their lips and tongue, as they are smaller movement. Essentially, under the effects of a strong adrenaline-dump survival stress response, the person's ability to put thoughts into words will be dimmed, and meanwhile their motor-skills (used to rapidly form shapes with your talking tools and your voice box) will deteriorate.

The phenomenon associated with this is the "look away and punch," which we have had described to us so many times in our training sessions:

"I was talking to the service user about this difficult decision we were trying to make together and then, after I raised a particularly contentious point, he suddenly went really quiet and turned away. Next thing I knew I was seeing stars—he punched me in the head!"

A person who is going to hurt you usually has to go through a process of dehumanising or de-personing you before they can do so. The look-away and the silence may be part of this.

You will observe: a quietening, a possible narrowing of focus, but away from you. They were talking, but now they are swallowing hard and they have "gone quiet." Be cautious.

Staring: "looking through you"

During a survival moment, your primal systems won't want to miss a moment of what's happening. It will shut off your blink reflex, widen your pupils, and dramatically increase your brain's visual data-processing speed so that you can literally see things that otherwise are not there. This effect can also

132

happen to a person who is seeing you as the threat, and they may fixate, pupils widening, appearing to be looking "right through you."

Some research was carried out many years ago into the personal safety practices of some night workers; their number one safety rule was to look out for the "thousand yard stare."

You will observe: a fixed gaze, looking "through" you or seeming to look in your direction, not necessarily at your eyes but at another part of your body. The person will be engaging you with their eyes but not conversationally.

Aggressive Gestures

Desmond Morris, the well-known author of books on human behaviour and body language expert, has described the use of the "finger baton" and its origins. In particular in situations where there is a difference of opinion, we see one or other person employing this gesture in order to emphasise their own point of view. It is a reasonably reliable indicator of how aroused the person is, being quite a primal and deep-level behaviour.

You will observe: a wagging or pointing finger, being used as a pseudo-weapon, brandished in front of your face and being directed towards you and/or the object of the conversation. It may from time to time also manifest as a fist, or the hand may be holding an object as an "improvised" weapon.

Broadcasting Body Language which enhances safety

When faced with an aggressive person who is presenting combative behaviour (such as any of those behaviours we looked at above)—shaking their fists, pacing and posturing to intimidate—then it is very important that you employ communication strategies which achieve two key objectives at the same time.

You want to:

1. Dissuade them from violence through your words and behaviour.
2. Position yourself in a way which enhances your safety.

Let's start with the first objective. What message do you want to send to the other person when they are aggressive and posturing? Well, because of our very unique behavioural approach to conflict management, we have conducted thousands of short, informal experiments with our groups over the years.

Here's how it goes. Myself as the instructor and a volunteer find themselves a space in the training room. We typically do not use a lot of space, and in fact, most of our training rooms for this exercise are quite busy areas, with desks and projectors, laptops, chairs and coats, bags of all descriptions all over the room. Much the same a most front rooms, bedrooms or hallways out there in the community.

My volunteer is always made aware of the possible nature of the exercise—I will be asking them to observe some of the physical signs of aggression noted in the previous section above. I am careful to allow the attendees to self-select for this activity, and I have been very fortunate to always have a willing volunteer in my groups!

The volunteer is asked to participate in an observation exercise. She must tell me in a moment what she sees, hears and feels while I present a display of behaviour to her. I tell her that, for safety, I am not allowed to touch her and she is not allowed to touch me. I am standing about 8-10 feet away, room permitting.

We begin. I break eye contact and begin to think of something which would make me very angry. I begin to look down at the floor and pace backwards and forwards. I raise my hand to my face and cover my eyes for a moment. I rub my head in my hands. This usually triggers a facial colour change. Meanwhile, I am huffing and puffing a little bit and my physical posture becomes tense as the chimpanzee inside tries to make me look bigger to my imagined opponent. Then, I slam my hand into a wall or a table and fix my eyes on my volunteer's eyes. I turn towards her and step decisively in her direction, a fixed stare now aimed right at her eyes.

I walk right up to my volunteer and if she doesn't move—most don't—I will get as close to a nose-to-nose contact without touching as I can.

At this point one of several things usually happens:

1. The volunteer breaks eye contact long before I get close and starts to giggle, while leaning away from me in any way she can, but not moving her feet.

2. The volunteer holds my eye contact and the proximity between us, steadfast and assertive.
3. The volunteer starts to step away while scanning me, her colleagues and her environment and denying me any proximity to her.

At this moment, the experiment completed, I take a big step backwards and present the biggest smile I can conjur up, telling the volunteer that the exercise is over and she can relax! This is very important—the stress involved in this 10-second exercise is palpable every time we do it, and not just for the volunteer!

Immediately, as I step backwards, I begin the debrief with the volunteer. How does she feel? What physical sensations? Very often the answers are:

- Heart beet feels noticeable and rapid
- Hands feel sweaty
- Tension in the body
- Rapid heating-up in the body

Depending on how intensely I have been able to present these aggressive behaviours to her, we have varying intensities of these feelings. It is worth noting, however, that even though this volunteer is in a training room with 10-12 of her colleagues, and that she is doing the exercise with an instructor who she has been present with for a few hours already, and she is fairly sure he is not going to hurt her (remember the no-touching rule?), none of this matters!

Fact versus Opinion

The survival brain—the chimpanzee inside—doesn't care for the constructs of safety or the fact. As a primal animal, it only cares about the impressions given off by what it sees in front of it right at that moment—the clenched fist, the pacing, the tension, the puffed-out chest, the red-face.

It essentially says, "To hell with your ideas of safety! There is an angry predator out there, and I am getting us ready to run or fight our way out of here!" You can't fool your survival system. It will act for you based on its assessment of risk, based on the things it can see, hear or smell.

Back to our experiment. We move on to a series of questions around observation and articulation. What, I ask the volunteer, did you see? About four times out of five the answers we get are as follows:

"You were upset and agitated; you were going to do something; I could see you were escalating and something was bothering you."

I then ask, "But what did you *actually see*?"

After a moment of consideration, we then get the factual observations:

"You were pacing and holding your hand to your face. Your colour changed. Your body went tense; your movement was jerky and stiff. You had a fixed gaze and looked straight through me. Your fist clenched and you walked right at me. You stepped into my space, very close. I felt uncomfortable."

When we write an expert opinion for a court, it is always important that we separate fact from opinion.

For example, if a worker in a real incident had faced these same behaviours and had decided to kick the aggressive person in the shin before turning to run to the door, then later on she would have to explain the reasoning of her actions to either her boss, to the police or to some other authority.

In this situation, it will be important for her to articulate honestly and specifically what she saw—the facts, as she believed them to be—that caused her to decide that the shin kick was necessary and proportionate. Her opinion will be important, however it will be clearer if she is able to articulate clearly the factual observations she made which caused her to form that opinion.

Pre-Cues

She may, given her level of knowledge, training and experience with physical violence, be able to articulate specific pre-cues which presage a physical assault. Examples of these pre-cues are the "pectoral twitch" associated with preparatory movements of the arm before a punch, or a sideways stance favouring the right side (like a tennis player getting ready to serve), which signals a preparation for large swinging blows, or the "witness glance" (also known as the "look-away-and-punch") when the aggressor does a last-second break of eye contact with the target.

Being aware of pre-cues is a vitally important part of Phase 3, the escalation phase. Research into the reaction times of elite athletes has found that the difference between novices and veterans in reacting to the movements of their opponents relies very specifically on their tacit awareness of the micro-adjustments their opponents are making before they complete even very sudden movements. Essentially, there are "tells" in other people's bodies which—even at critical speeds such as we see in sports or in combat—can make a difference in response time.

Proximity

In our experiment, the next question to the volunteer is, "Did you want to move during the exercise? In which direction?" The answer is almost always the same. "Yes. I wanted to step backwards."

Good. This is good practice—following your intuition. Any time your intuition or instinct wants you to step away from an angry or aggressive person, you should follow it— immediately!

Of course every now and then we meet a very experienced volunteer who has perhaps been working with a certain client group which thrives on manipulation and confrontation. Sometimes these workers tell us that they will not step backwards or step away from these clients, as it would signal weakness or "losing." We acknowledge that this may, in very rare cases, be the best way to deal with aggressive behaviour and that you may develop a specific strategy for a specific person or situation which requires this "assertive strategy."

Bear with me right now while we explore a more generic role of proximity management and body language presentation; we can return to special circumstances later.

One variation of this experiment is to have our instructor step up to a very close (nose-to-nose) proximity with the volunteer once more and ask, "How does this feel?"

Invariably, hyper-proximity is uncomfortable, unpleasant, weird, unnerving and noxious. Quite naturally, we try to keep

139

noxious substances at a distance. We do this mainly by stepping away from them, and in the case of a noxious human being, we do this carefully, by stepping away from them while maintaining the ability to watch their behaviour—stepping backwards, not turning around.

How else do we manage proximity?

Well, you could ask my three-year-old. Let me explain. If I put some lettuce on a fork and then slowly move it towards my three-year-old's face, explaining to her that green foods are good for her and that she should try it, what behaviour do you think I would observe?

Well, here's what happens:

- She quickly notices the "noxious stimulus" in her visual field.

- Her hand disengages from whatever she is holding on to.

- Her shoulders raise.

- The hand closest to the noxious object begins to move up in front of her face.

- Her palm turns away from her body and towards the object.

- As her hand nears her face, it changes direction and starts to extend towards the object.

- Meanwhile, her entire body is leaning away from the object.

- Finally, when the object is at close proximity, she will turn her head away from the object.

- Often, the eye closest to the object will squeeze shut.

...and then we stay there until the lettuce goes away or I negotiate a deal about ice cream!

The point I am trying to make about how we manage proximity as human beings is that no one taught my daughter to move this way. What I described to you is a natural pattern of movements designed to keep bad things physically at a distance from us, and it is hard-wired into our nervous system.

> **"A basic function of the motor system of all animals is to protect the body from attack or collision."**
>
> *Parieto-frontal interactions, personal space,*
> *and defensive behavior*
> —Michael S.A. Graziano, Dylan F. Cooke 2005

Back to our experiment and the next question I ask to my volunteer. "Now that your feet are moving you away from me, what else can you do to keep me physically at a distance?" At once, our groups raise their hands in front of their bodies.

The Barrier Signal

As I look around the room, I see a huge variation in hand positions, postures, attitudes and signaling.

There are:

- Fully-extended arms, pushed all the way to their extreme range of motion;

- Compressed arm positions, with the hands just in front of the chest;

- "Surrender" positions with the person's hands placed back and away from their bodies or overhead;

- "Kato" from the pink panther ("karate hands")—most popular with male attendees;

- The "X-Factor," with forearms crossed in front of the body (sometimes with fists); and

- The single-arm fully extended in front of the body.

There is, however, one commonality between all of these gestures: the open palm. I look around the room and asked the attendees what this open palm means.

"Stop," the chorus rings out in every training room I've been in for hundreds of training groups. This signal—the upraised open hand, fingers splayed and palm pointed forwards—appears to be one of the most universal devices of non-verbal communication available to us. (*In only one case did a young man who was exercising his intellect too far call out, "It means Five!" which earned him my close attention for the rest of the day!*)

Remember my three-year-old? When she becomes aware of a noxious stimulus in her field of awareness, her palm opens and rushes to intercept it, keep it at a distance. Now, in a room full of adults, when I ask them what this gesture means, I have a universal interpretation: "Stop."

We then proceed to talk to staff about where this stop position needs to be placed and how. For example, should your "Stop" signal be telling the person that:

1. You are afraid they are going to hurt you?

2. You are willing and able to hurt them?

3. You are submitting to their control of the incident?

4. You are not engaging with them?

Clearly, there are certain ways we can display and broadcast body language which does not assist us to professionally engage with clients. Signalling the fully extended arm position is dismissive and disengaging. Signalling the "surrender" position is ceding control of the discussion to the other person, letting them know that they are running things. Signalling the shallow, hands-next-to-chest position doesn't protect your personal space or enhance your safety. Signalling that you have one hand "ready" to strike out with predisposes the negotiation to include the threat of violence.

So, what is our recommendation?

Well, we have to arrive at a good compromise between communicating professional engagement and the need to maintain a safe perimeter within which we can move and think.

Enter the Barrier Signal

These are the criteria for our "standard model" barrier signal:

- Hands Open, at chest height
- Fingers open and splayed
- Palms forward (pointing towards the person)
- Elbows bent so that your arm is about two-thirds extended

One key point here is that your arms, while you display this Barrier Signal, should move in a relaxed, conversational way. They should not be stiff or static. Remember, you are talking with your hands!

Once you are happy with this posture (yes, you should step in front of a mirror and try it on for size!), then I want you to add in some other elements.

The first element I want you to add in is a "slow down" gesture. How do you tell someone to slow down with your hands? Perhaps by moving your hands, slowly and smoothly, in an up-and-down space in front of your body, so as to model how you want them to move. Careful now, they are not on fire. You are not trying to put them out by smothering flames! The movement is smaller and more subtle than that! With practice, you will find that by using this motion you can suggest to the person you are talking with that you want them to slow down.

In my own practice, I will also often, ever so slightly, cock my head to one side (listening signal) so as to show the person that I am trying hard to listen to what they are saying.

The combination of Proximity, Open Palms, Slow-Down Gesture and the Listening Signal should all lend your high-stakes conversation a quality of safety and professionalism, compared to a situation where you do not employ them.

The reason I am going into such detail about this Barrier Signal skill with you is that I would like for you to have this intelligent tool at your disposal in any conflict scenario. I want you to be able to flick an internal switch that is labelled "Body Language for Conflict" so that your body will begin this level of communication without further conscious thought.

Once you grasp the essential elements here: Proximity, Open Palms, Slow-Down Gesture, Listening Signal, and then I want you to practice and apply them in varying degrees, depending on the scenario you are in. Each element has an inflection and a tone which can change according to circumstances.

For example, you might want to do the "standard model" Barrier Signal above and then play with it by leaning. Lean forward—what does this communicate to the person? Lean backward—how does this communicate some other message?

Perhaps this universally recognised sign is based on universal behaviour, such as that observed by Graziano in his studies of monkeys and their protective gestures?

Stimulation [by a threatening or looming stimulus] evokes a constellation of movements, including blinking, squinting, flattening the ear against the side of the head, shifting the head away from the sensory receptive fields, shrugging the shoulder, and rapidly lifting the hand into the space near the side of the head as if to block an impending impact.

Stimulation of this type...evoked movements consistent with defending the side of the head from an impending threat. These movements included a squint and facial grimace that was more pronounced on the side of the sensory receptive field, a turning of the head away from the side of the sensory receptive field, a rapid movement of the hand to an upper lateral location as if blocking an object in the sensory receptive field, and a turning outward of the palm.

Defensive Movements Evoked in Monkeys
—Cooke et al. 2003; Graziano et al. 2002

Aggressive Gestures

As we have signals like the "Stop" gesture and "Slow Down" gesture noted above, it is also possible that we have inbuilt motor programs for displaying anger and aggression.

In our sessions, to facilitate accurate replication of real events during role-plays, we need all our role players to be able to convincingly display body language which tells the other person how they are feeling.

We ask them to practice our "standard model" of aggressive postures:

- The pointy finger
- The shaking fist
- The surprise gesture
- Head-in-hands

Having reviewed many CCTV and available videos of non-consensual fighting, where one person is actively pushing the fight onto the other person, these four main aggressive gesture behaviours are very evident in the pre-assault phase. They are highly predictable in the period of time when there is close proximity between the participants in a heated disagreement, and therefore they form a core part of our training.

Now, having completed both sides of the body-language conundrum, we can put the aggressor and the defuser together and see what happens!

ROLE PLAY:
Aggressor: Pointy Finger, Shaking Fist, surprise gesture, head-in-hands (cycling these).
Defuser: Barrier Signals, Managing Proximity, Listening, Moving towards safety.

Tracking, Shock-Absorbing and the Patrick Swayze Rule
As this increasingly realistic role-play now progresses, we see another issue develop. As the aggressor's hands, fingers and fists begin to appear in close proximity to the defuser's body,

there appears a very urgent need to "deal with" these potential threats.

Most people will begin to look panicked and will start to mirror the aggressor's movement at this time, darting their hands forward and back, left and right in order to counter the person's motion in an effort at "blocking" them. However, we use the word "barrier" very carefully to describe this set of skills.

We encourage the defuser to now address the aggressor's movements by doing three things:

- Manage proximity at all times (applying the "Patrick Swayze" rule).
- Use your hands as barriers, obstructing physical access to you.
- Absorb any collision in a pliable way.

In *that* famous movie, Patrick Swayze's character is desperately trying to teach his protégé not to get herself tangled up in his dirty dancing. In an effort to keep her from tripping him up, he says these important words:

"THIS is my dance-space (gesturing to the area in front of him)*, and that* (gesturing to the area in front of his partner) *is your dance-space."*

So we ask you to do the same with your barrier signal! Use those palms and your almost-extended arms to delineate your own personal space. This is a space that no one should enter without invitation or permission.

This is the "Patrick Swayze rule"—manage proximity!

As the person moves their hands around in the space in front of your body, you should not mirror them, but merely and continually place your hands in a position in which you are obstructing their access (quietly, subtly) to your body and from which you can move to protect yourself from any kind of impact they can deliver.

This is a skill best taught in person, but it can be taught quickly and easily. Starting in the right position—a position which enhances safety and delays the onset of physical violence—may be far more important than knowing 25 different escapes from disadvantageous positions when everything has gone terribly wrong!

Anyone who has ever sited, designed and built a castle probably focussed primarily on seeing their aggressors coming from a long way away to give the defenders time to prepare. Then, they likely focussed on making their fortress difficult to penetrate. If the walls fail, they still have a plan, but they want to build the walls strong in any case! Your barrier signal is your castle wall; make it difficult to penetrate.

Your barrier signal is designed to present a professional face to the aggressive person while you attempt to defuse the situation. Its secondary purpose is to slow down the descent into violence by making you a comparatively harder target.

In this we have good anecdotal evidence from our own practice, our colleagues and our trainees that the deployment of a barrier signal during high-stakes conflict scenarios actually does slow down the progression towards violence. The combination of the broadcasted "stop," "slow-down" and "listening" gestures, the management of proximity and the covert obstructions offered by the Patrick Swayze rule all serve one critical purpose: **to give you more time to talk and more time to think, while making it difficult for the other person to make contact.**

Managing Proximity and Using Barrier Signals

Proximity Drill: Hands as Barriers

Aggressive client closes proximity with the Lone Worker.

**When Lone Worker feels the right time has come,
they begin to raise arms.**

Aggressive Client continues to close proximity. Lone Worker takes a step backward to maintain distance.

Aggressive Client continues to close proximity. Lone Worker presents a strong barrier signal while stepping backwards.

Drill complete after 3-4 steps backwards.

Managing Aggressive Gestures

Pointing Finger

Shaken fist

Hands out to the side

Hands on top of head

Barrier Drill

Aggressive Client closes proximity with Lone Worker.

**Lone Worker begins to employ Barrier Signal
and Stepping Back.**

Aggressive Client cycles through Aggressive Gestures. Lone Worker now orients their arm positions in response to Aggressive Client's arm movements.

Lone Worker moves hands towards the shaken fist, presenting a barrier

Toward the pointed finger, presenting a barrier. Keep the arms out from the body, not allowing them to collapse.

Lone Worker raises hands to present a barrier to the Aggressive Client's higher position of hands

Lone Worker lowers hands slightly and spreads them out to present a barrier to Aggressive Client's outspread arms.

Of course, the Barrier Signal's third purpose is to put you in a good position to actively protect yourself and deploy a breakaway strategy, using reasonable force as a last resort, to get out of a situation. This is the focus of our next chapter.

Further reading for this chapter:

Morris, D	*The Human Zoo*	Vintage, 1994
Morris, D	*The Naked Ape*	Corgi Books, 1967
Morris, D	*Manwatching - A Field guide to Human Behaviour*	Grafton Books, 1997
Ekman, P	*Emotions Revealed - Understanding Faces and Feelings*	Phoenix, 2003
Winston, R	*Human Instinct - How our primeval impulses shape our modern lives*	Bantam Books, 2002
Tallis, R	*Michelangelo's Finger*	Atlantic Books, 2010

Chapter 8:

Reasonable Force

It is possible that your efforts to defuse and disengage are unsuccessful, and that the person you are interacting with becomes extremely aggressive to the point of physical violence.

At this time it may be necessary for you to physically protect yourself from attack. The law allows for such a use of force—to protect against physical violence—and social care or healthcare workers should make themselves familiar with the rules which apply.

The rapid decision making which is involved in using force to restrain or to break away from another person may be confused by rumour, hearsay and inference, usually derived from media stories which cloud the issues. Care workers in particular—because of their beliefs and values—are susceptible to erroneous beliefs about their rights to protect themselves and prevent their clients coming to harm.

Let's take some time to look at the issues here.

10 questions about using reasonable force

1: Am I allowed to defend myself if a client attacks me?

Everyone has the right to protect themselves from unlawful physical violence. In Mark Dawes excellent book entitled *Understanding Reasonable Force*, the history and key principles of UK laws in regard to offences against the person and the defence of self-defence in relation to assault are explained very clearly.

I don't want to reproduce the very robust explanation provided by Mark Dawes here, but I do recommend it to the interested reader.

Instead, we will produce a broad decision making framework which is based on the legal interpretations outlined in *Understanding Reasonable Force*.

Situations in which you may use force

Every person has the right to use "Reasonable Force" in certain circumstances. These circumstances include when one is being assaulted, mugged, threatened with harm and so on, and circumstances where you are genuinely trying to prevent or stop a crime from being committed.

As the concept of "freedom" is central to our society, and any restriction of freedom is quite a serious matter in law, there also exists a lawful excuse to use reasonable force to prevent one's freedom from being taken away unlawfully. In simple terms, if, for example, someone tries to lock you in a room or building, and you want to get out, but they won't let you leave, then there may be a case for you to use reasonable force against that person to remove yourself from that situation.

Circumstances

The law generally allows people to use force as long as it is "reasonable in the circumstances." What this means is that a discussion of exactly what the circumstances of the incident were will be very central to any decision about whether the use of force was justified.

Example of an Attack:

A person reaches out to a lone worker and grabs his shirt with both hands, pushing and jostling the worker about. In response to these actions, the worker steps back to gain their balance and then kicks their leg in a powerful blow to the other person's shin, causing them to fall to the floor. The attacker lets go.

Does this sound like a reasonable response?

Well, the truth is that you *can't* answer whether it was reasonable or not, because you have *no idea of what the actual circumstances were!*

Where did this happen?

Who was involved?

Who exactly was the attacker?

What happened immediately prior to the grab?

What were they saying to each other when the grab happened?

Why did the person grab onto the lone worker?

How powerful was the grip (was it painful, unbalancing, slamming the worker into a wall?)

How quickly was this incident unfolding?

Scenario 1:

John works visiting older people who need support at home. A client in their home beckons John over to where he is sitting. As John leans in close to talk to the resident, the client reaches out of his chair and grabs John by the shirt with both hands while pleading, "Please! I'm absolutely parched; can you bring me some water?"

Scenario 2:

Jane works visiting vulnerable people with drug and alcohol problems. During a night visit to a well-known client, the client's friend forcibly enters the flat and grabs the client by his clothing. He slams the client into the wall, headbutts him in the face, breaking the client's nose and knocking him unconscious and bleeding, to the floor. He then turns to Jane and grabs her by her shirt with both hands saying, "I'll kill you too!"

Reasonable Response?

Now, in which case is the kick to the shin potentially a reasonable response in the circumstances?

It's all about the Circumstances!

This is central: the circumstances will always help you—and the courts where necessary—to determine what a reasonable response might be. This is key (and missed by many)—the typology of the attack ("a grab") is not sufficient for us to determine what the response should be. Only the scenario and the circumstances can assist us in determining what an appropriate response might be, both tactically and legally.

Breakaway and self-defence training providers should take particular note here, as we are well aware of "packages" of training which likely serve to increase risk rather than to reduce it because of the erroneous way in which they categorise certain attacks.

In the example above the clothing grab is common to both scenarios; however, the level of risk in each scenario is vastly different.

Many workers whom we have spoken to at courses have told us that they believe there is some requirement "out there" in the world which binds them to carry out an "ideal" response to a physical assault. But because the circumstances of every assault are different, the responses to them which might be reasonable can be hugely varied.

In our experience, having carried out thousands of replicated assault scenarios using full protective gear and in varying conditions, we believe that there exists no "ideal" response to the chaotic nature of any physical assault, except in theory! There are optimal and less optimal approaches, but there is no single technique or tactic that can be matched and declared "suitable" for every vaguely described scenario.

Remember, the requirement of the law is that the person defending themselves does what is "reasonable in the circumstances." There is no rule which mandates you do the "ideal" thing!

Last Resort

There appears, however, one overriding theme about a justified use of force: the requirement that if force is used, it is the "last resort." In any case where a court must examine a use of force and decide whether or not it was justified, you can expect that there will be quite an exhaustive discussion about whether or not the person had alternatives to the use of force at the time they acted.

For example, the person who gets into a fight in front of an open doorway is quite likely to be asked (and tested) about whether or not they could have somehow used the open doorway to exit the situation, or whether they could have used the door as a barrier to prevent the conflict, rather than getting into the fight.

Could the person have somehow defused the situation verbally, or did they have time and space to disengage and make some physical withdrawal?

Necessary, or believed to be necessary

The law allows for only necessary lawful action in defence of oneself (or another person).

If the person could defuse the situation verbally, or they could withdraw, or shut a door temporarily to avoid the situation, then it could be said that that action was all that was necessary for them to do and nothing more was needed.

When confronted, if the person can use time and space to avoid the need to use force on the other person, then, in our peaceful and civilised society, this is the action that is expected to have been taken, rather than resorting to violence.

In summary, when a person is in imminent danger and when efforts to defuse or disengage from a situation have failed, or there is no chance for them to take effect, then it may be necessary for the worker to act.

Wherever the person is seen to have acted without necessity, then it may be said that the reason they used force on the other person was:

- To take revenge

- To retaliate against the person

- To teach them a lesson (retribution)

- To simply make them comply with an order

- For convenience

In any of these situations, it will be very difficult for the person to use the "reasonable force" defence and ask the court to excuse their actions.

Perception of events

It is worth noting that there is provision in both English and Scottish law for a principle known as "honestly held belief," which allows for the person's perception of the unfolding event to determine whether they feel it is necessary to act.

In English law it is called "honestly held belief" and in Scots law it is said that even a mistaken belief, if honest and reasonable, would function as a defence, because "some allowances must be made...for the state of fear or the heat in the blood at the moment of the man who is attacked."

As an example of just how a person's perception can be heightened, or altered, in a situation of grave risk, one need only peruse some of the recollections of life-threatening scenarios explored by David Klinger or Alexis Artwohl. In *Into the Kill Zone* for example, police officers in life-and-death use of force encounters relate seeing their incidents unfolding in slow motion, or in high-contrast colour, or with exceptional clarity of sight or hearing, or with serious distortions in their senses or thought processes.

The person's own implicit perception—their snap-judgement—of the incident as it unfolds is an important factor in determining whether a use of force was necessary.

When a use of force is necessary, how much force to use?

The standard applied here is called Proportionality. Were the actions taken proportionate to the harm to be avoided or the evil to be avoided, or the crime to be prevented?

If the actions were necessary (see above) **and** the force used then prevented a greater harm from occurring in those circumstances, then the chances are that it was a proportionate response to the situation that was unfolding.

Exercise in proportionality

Lone workers who escort their service users into the community on excursions sometimes have to deal with the risk of their service user ignoring traffic safety and running out onto a busy road.*

IF you were walking with a client near a busy main road and suddenly the client shouted at a friend of theirs across the road and went to run between traffic to talk to her, would you be justified in that moment in holding the client and pulling them away from the busy road?

Would this situation pose an imminent danger to the client?
What opportunity exists to "talk the client out of it"?
What if the client fell over and broke their wrist as a result of your hold?

Did your actions (even with the injury) still prevent a worse kind of harm from happening?

* What Risk Assessment issues does this raise?

- Staffing numbers with this client?

- Training required if the client needs to be prevented from running onto roads?

- Planning the excursion location?

Other examples of proportionality in action:

- Police using a Taser to incapacitate a mentally-ill man who is experiencing a psychotic episode (with super-human strength and endurance) and is violently assaulting police officers.

- A 44-year-old female care staff using a pain-inducing wrist-lock to control an 18 year-old, 6 ft. tall young man, who is trying to punch another client in the face.

- A woman who is threatened with being mugged at knifepoint kicks her attacker in the shin and breaks his leg.

2: Am I allowed to protect someone else if they are attacked by a client?

The law allows for you to defend yourself or another person against unlawful physical violence, so this covers your colleagues and also your client.

Note also our previous chapter about Duty of Care under the Health and Safety at Work Act, where we discussed how this act places an obligation on team members at work to take reasonable care for themselves and others.

3: If I cause an injury or a bruise, is it abuse?

In 1996, the Crown Prosecution Service issued a memorandum about the issues arising out of a situation where a person uses reasonable force which then results in an injury. It reads as follows:

Particular care must be taken in dealing with cases of assault where the allegation is made by a "victim" who was, at the time, engaged in criminal activity himself. For instance, a burglar who claims to have been assaulted by the occupier of the premises concerned.

Where the use of force in any of these circumstances is reasonable, the "assailant" has an absolute defence and charges relating to the assault should not be brought.

—CPS Offences Against the Person Charging Standard, 26 April 1996

From this we may observe a fundamental premise of the law, that reasonable force is, by definition, both necessary and proportionate and therefore cannot also constitute the "wrong thing to do."

In fact, it seems altogether reasonable to acknowledge that during any rapidly unfolding conflict scenario where there is force used, then bruising, abrasions and contusions can be expected. Even if the person who is bruised or injured is a "vulnerable" person, this does not automatically mean abuse has occurred.

As I often mention to my training groups, the only way to absolutely guarantee that physical intervention will not leave a bruise would be to have some kind of mystical "Jedi" powers that allow people to move objects without physical contact. The serious point here is that we must be realistic about the use of physical force between people. It is never pretty. It is never tidy or neat. It is never fully predictable for anyone involved. It is sometimes a chaotic collision of bodies which lasts until one party overpowers the other one long enough to be decisive in ending the conflict.

Not unlike a surgeon making an incision, you as a healthcare or community worker, may need to make a carefully calculated intervention in order to bring about a comparatively better outcome for your client.

4: Do I need to be trained before I can restrain or use force in self-defence?

The rights and responsibilities of using force for protection are granted to every person equally under the rules of reasonable force as described above. There is no way that an employer can remove these rights; any person faced with potential harm may act when necessary according to their honestly held belief and then in a proportionate manner to protect themselves or another person.

No policy maker should apply other, more stringent, rules about the use of force, as that could constitute a breach of staff rights granted to them under very well-established common and statute law.

The requirement to train staff in methods of restraint, intervention or self-defence and breakaway comes from the Health & Safety at Work Act 1974, where the employers' duties to enable their staff to work in safety are set out. As we have explained above, Section 2 of this act explicitly states that the employer has the responsibility to train staff to carry out their work safely. The responsibility to have training is not the employees.

5: What can I do if the client locks me in somewhere?

In meeting thousands of lone workers over the years, I have observed that in a training room where I meet 12-15 reasonably experienced staff, I can be sure of hearing at least one story where a person has been locked into a house or a room during a conflict scenario. Often it is a measure of last resort for the client, who desperately wants to continue a discussion about some decision they wish to negotiate. In these cases, the locking or barring of a door is a gambit to prolong the negotiation and find some control within their difficult situation.

From time to time though, the detention of the lone worker is a calculated or deliberate action made in order to intimidate the worker or threaten the worker's safety.

Freedom is a central idea within our system of society and is heavily protected within the law. It follows easily then that the law allows us to use reasonable force in order to prevent or terminate the unlawful detention of ourselves.

Illustration:

I once met a community mental health nurse who told me the following story:

> *"I arrived at my client, Jimmy's house as scheduled, in order to check that he had attended hospital for his medication. As soon as I arrived I noticed that he was sweating profusely and his presentation was rather erratic. He greeted me at the door and hurriedly ushered me inside the house.*
>
> *After trying to exchange some usual pleasantries, I asked if he had attended the clinic that morning to have his medication. This prompted a stream of angry ranting about how the doctors and nurses at the clinic were trying to control his mind and steal his thoughts.*
>
> *I acknowledged that he was very upset and offered my excuses, having decided quickly that I wanted to leave the house. Before I could react, Jimmy rushed to the front door and locked it. When I protested that I wanted to leave, Jimmy told me that, for my own protection, he wouldn't let me go because "they" would then get me!*
>
> *Deciding that I had time on my side, I took a seat on the couch in the living room and asked Jimmy to make me a cup of tea, seeing as we were going to have to wait a while to get this all sorted out.*
>
> *I was relaxed at this point, because I myself had written our lone working safety policy, and I knew that the protocols demanded that the office would call me 30 minutes from the beginning of*

the appointment time. I settled onto the sofa with my cup of tea and biscuit, with my mobile phone on the armrest.

Two hours later and faced with escalating behaviour from the client, I realised that any hope of a call from the office was now a forlorn hope. My mobile did not ring; Jimmy was sweating and his behaviour was becoming increasingly impulsive and paranoid. He was no longer listening to me. It was getting dark outside.

That's when I did it.

I stood up off the sofa. I put him on his ass [sic.], and I threw a chair through the window of his front room. I jumped through the hole it created and ran like the clappers to my car.

I know I did the right thing that day, but the decision was a hard one.

Jimmy had a history of serious violence when he was feeling unwell, and I had waited as long as I could for help to come. He was no longer responding to my efforts at conversation. He was losing control.

To this day, I clearly remember thinking, as I ran to my car that it was going to cost me a pretty penny to replace the glass in Jimmy's front-room window!"

Safe Systems of Work Review Questions from previous Chapter:

How does your team manage where you are and whether you are safe?

Do you use an In/Out board?

Do you use the "Buddy System" of calls amongst workers?

Does someone at your office have responsibility to call you during your visits?

Do you have responsibility to call in during your shifts? At the end of your shifts?

Can, or do you, use technology to assist this?

Does everyone in your team comply with the systems in place?

6: If I have to use force on a client, are there "approved techniques" that I should use?

No. The only applicable rule is whether or not you used Reasonable Force in the circumstances. One of the purposes of self-defence/breakaway or physical intervention training is to give staff a broader range of alternatives to the primal survival and fighting behaviours which are part of our genetic inheritance. Trainers should guide staff in using simple, gross-motor techniques which are accessible under stress and which can be proportionate in many different scenarios.

There are, however, also other and often old school approaches to training which are less desirable.

A number of studies are openly available which have sought to determine the effectiveness of breakaway training to staff. In the main these have been conducted in the healthcare sector, where it is common for staff to have mandatory "Breakaway" training, so called because its primary aim is to enable the staff to disengage from an assault.

Studies from Parkes (1996), Southcott (2002 and 2007), Avon & Wiltshire Mental Health Partnership Trust (2009), Dobson

171

(2008), Wright (2005), the Royal College of Psychiatrists (2005) and Rogers (2006) have begun to raise serious questions about the focus, efficacy and methodology of breakaway training for staff.

These studies have tended to find:

1. Staff are attacked by "kinetic" assaults (punching and kicking) predominantly.

2. Many staff feel they don't have time to respond adequately to the assault.

3. Many staff don't or can't execute the breakaway technique they have been taught.

In fact, in Rogers' study, 60% of staff failed to apply the "correct" technique, even when they were told beforehand what the specific attack was that the simulated aggressor was going to use on them! Crucially, Rogers observed 40% of the staff in his study as being unable to break away from a life-threatening assault in under 10 seconds.

In another study of efficacy at St Andrews by Dickens et al. (2009), it was found that only 14% of staff were able to use the correct breakaway technique. However, 80% of people did manage to get away from the assault even though they did not use the techniques taught.

This prompted one commentator to observe that perhaps instinctive human behaviour was more likely to have success than the training system which the staff were required to learn!

Breakaway and Disengagement Tactics

At Dynamis, when we teach Breakaway and Disengagement tactics to staff, we utilise a method of training known as "Behavioural Self Protection." Its premise is that natural human movement and the survival system's built-in responses are highly reliable, easy to learn, and are compatible with what people with very little training will do anyway in a life-threatening situation. In our experience, these methods can be taught quickly and are retained more easily.

From our perspective as trainers and advisers, it would appear that many training organisations around the UK may in fact be increasing their level of liability and risk by ignoring or failing to heed the increasingly available and established information about how people perform learned motor skills under the high levels of stress and in the chaotic mobile geometry of a real confrontation.

Our friend and colleague, Mark Dawes, from the National Federation for Personal Safety—one of the few expert witnesses on use-of-force in the UK—has used widely acknowledged and well-known scientific evidence about motor skill acquisition and performance to demonstrate how training providers may have been negligent by designing and delivering their training contrary to this information.

Does Breakaway training reflect this?

My favourite example of this is when we talk to people about hair grabs from service users. What is the actual risk from a hair grab? Of course it depends on the circumstances; however, in so many Breakaway courses the "bad guy" role player simply stands there, extends his hand and politely holds the person's hair.

In reality though, the hair grab is often part of something we call a compound attack. It is an assault that starts with a threat, then a shove, a hair grab and then pulling the person or pushing them into a bad position, which then enables the "bad-guy" to deliver blows or kicks to them easily.

This "chain" of attacks, compounding one another, is more likely to be the real process of a violent assault than the static scenario which is designed in to the watered-down training packages I have seen in many NHS, Local Authority, Prison Service and other programmes.

In my experience too many programmes are either watered down so much as to act in two main and desperately less-desirable ways. The skills presented either underwhelm the staff to such a degree that the tactics shown are immediately dismissed as "useless," or else the virtually "useless" skills that have been designed into the course are presented with such charm and charisma as to instill over-confidence in the trainees to the point that they are ready to take on anyone!

On these courses—of either variety above—huge amounts of time are often devoted to the study of how to break out of wrist-holds! So much so that the staff must go home to their partners, friends and loved-ones and say, "Go ahead, grab my wrist, I dare ya!"

However, we know that over 50% of the most serious assaults recorded against healthcare staff are kinetic assaults, i.e. punches and kicks.

Please choose your training provider with great care if you venture into the area of breakaway and self-defence/self-protection training. They should be able to:

- Show you a recognised accreditation in self-protection instruction from a credible source

- Evidence their training programme with reference to well-established sports science

- Teach a minimal number of key tactics (we teach <u>two</u> physical "frames" which can be used in the most critical self-defence scenarios, for example)

- Demonstrate an understanding of what really happens in a physical confrontation

In an effort to help our client agencies to examine the systems they are using and to begin to incorporate more modern approaches to the training of their staff, our team has compiled a list of issues which we suggest should be covered by a robust and resilient breakaway/self-defence system of work.

A robust Breakaway and Self Protection or Self Defence system of work will have the following attributes:

- **Explains how survival stress impacts on perception**
- **Explains how changes in arousal affect physical performance**
- **Improving Reaction Time is addressed by the training**
- **The training system addresses Stimulus Identification**
- **The training system addresses Stimulus-Response Compatibility**

- **Reflexive movements and defensive gestures are intrinsic to the training system**
- **The skills being learned are "low-maintenance"**
- **Simple solutions are preferred over complex ones within the training system**
- **The system uses what the learner can do, rather than what they must learn to do**
- **Progressive Intensity and Desirable Difficulties are introduced in training**
- **Some stress-exposure and stress-inoculation is achieved in the training**
- **The training system addresses intrinsic performer issues (motivation etc.)**

7: Do I have to wait until I have been struck / shoved / kicked / grabbed before I take action?

The law generally recognises that a person who is in imminent danger of being physically assaulted does not need to wait until the blow has landed, or the knife has cut, or an injury received before they take necessary defensive action.

Pre-Emptive Strike

This principle of the "pre-emptive strike" is well established in law: a person who perceives an imminent physical attack may use force first, as long as they have been attempting to defuse, disengage and otherwise show an unwillingness to engage in the fight in the first place and their action is a last resort.

This seems very applicable to many of the situations I hear about from lone workers in threatening situations. Often the worker from health or social care is attempting to defuse high-stress situations when the client crosses the threshold from rage to violence. Where this process is visible, and the worker can discern the client's descent towards violence, then a rapid, timely physical intervention may indeed be the most prudent course of action.

This is especially the case where there is a difference in the relative athleticism of those involved. For example, if the aggressor is much heavier or stronger than the worker, then waiting until after they have struck, before initiating defensive action is actually going to be less desirable for the worker's safety and security.

The Pre-Emptive strike may be a low-level intervention, such as a push or shove which increases the person's chance of success in getting to the exit-door, or it may be an action taken to keep a drawer full of knives firmly shut; both are examples of pre-emptive uses of force which do not require any "Jackie Chan" levels of coordination, timing or balance to achieve!

8: Who should investigate a use of force incident?

9: Who ultimately decides whether I did the right thing or the wrong thing?

Where there is a serious doubt that a use of force has been reasonable (and therefore the implication that a staff member committed an assault), then serious consideration should be given to whether the police should be asked to investigate the incident. Only a full investigation of relevant evidence— presented to the police, then the prosecution service (or procurator fiscal) and finally then in a court of law—can ultimately decide whether a use of force was reasonable.

Having been involved in some cases where it has happened, I feel it is doubtful that, left in the hands of a board of governors, a team manager, a supervisor, a Care Commission or an OF-STED inspector, that an incident involving the issues discussed in this chapter will be dealt with strictly and only according to principles of criminal law which apply to a case of alleged assault and the use of reasonable force.

Health and Social care workers and managers have more often developed expertise in family law and medical or care legislation than they have developed an awareness of the issues discussed in this chapter. We recommend that in the event of an incident of violence or use-of-force, staff seek competent authorities to assist in investigating any incident of violence and the use of force involved to make it safe.

Of course when we talk about restraint interventions (as opposed to self-defence interventions) the Metal Capacity Act 2005 (and the Adults with Incapacity Act 2005 in Scotland) have a bearing on decision making; however, these are typically concerned with the management of issues of capacity relating to foreseeable events which can be planned for. Furthermore, it is important to note that the central principles which relate to restraint and intervention in those pieces of legislation contain and encapsulate the core principles of "Reasonable Force" anyway.

Note that the Employment Rights Act 1994 Section 100 specifically states that an employee cannot be dismissed for taking appropriate steps to protect themselves or another person from serious or imminent danger. The Common Law and Criminal Law says that using "Reasonable Force" is an appropriate step to take in protecting people from harm, or preventing or terminating crime or when resisting being detained unlawfully.

Recent government guidance in the education sector has clarified the position on "Reasonable Force," underlining the rights of staff in caring positions to make physical interventions to prevent harm and advising that they should be able to make decisions about the use of force with the firm knowledge that they will be supported by their management.

10: What's the alternative to using force?

According to the rules laid out above, the use of force should always be a last resort. This means that staff must always be looking for alternatives to physical solutions in conflict scenarios.

Alternatives include:

- Disengaging (by leaving the situation)
- Containing (by isolating the threat physically, i.e. shutting a door)
- Defusing (by listening and talking)

However, if no other option exists then we must allow the option for staff to use force to protect themselves or colleagues or to safeguard clients.

How far will you go?

Emotionally, most social and healthcare workers have an aversion to using force to resolve a conflict situation. This is as it should be, and it is totally consistent with the ethos and values of a caring service professional.

However, when faced with imminent or present violence, and when in danger of being hurt or suffering a life-threatening or life-changing injury, it is natural to expect the worker to take reasonable steps to protect themselves. During our sessions, we often meet a worker who finds difficulty with this concept. They sometimes argue using moral or ethical reasons for acting always in the "best interests" of their "vulnerable" clients.

For those workers who find difficulty with the idea of using force on a client, even in circumstances where their own life may be endangered, we offer the following paradigm shifts:

Mathematics Problem:
In a room where one human being with dementia /learning disabilities/addiction/mental ill-health/challenging behaviour/ anger problems/temporary rage threatens violent behaviour towards a social care worker, how many vulnerable people are actually in the room?

Our answer: Two vulnerable people!

1 x vulnerable human being who lacks capacity /control/ awareness

1 x vulnerable human being who is being physically assaulted

Human Rights
The protection of your life is the most fundamental human right you possess under Article 2. It says that, "Everyone's right to life shall be protected by law." The government is compelled by the positive obligation to preserve life embodied in Article 2 and to uphold your rights; the legal framework in the United Kingdom allows for the use of force to protect your life.

What would your family say?

If you don't protect your life, or you suffer some terrible injury, what does your family stand to lose? An important income? A career ruined when you are left unable to work? A lifetime spent unable to carry your shopping, or your children? A mother, a father, a daughter or son?

Upholding your duty of care

If you allowed your client to commit a criminal act and hurt or injure you, then did you truly uphold your duty of care to protect and safeguard them from all forms of harm?

For any or all of these reasons, how far will you go? How little time will you hesitate?

NHS Carer left permanently scarred by attacks from patients

A former health worker has been awarded £825,000 damages after she was repeatedly punched, stamped and bitten by patients. Lisa Carter, 38, was left with permanent neck damage and is unable to fully use her right arm.

She was the victim of a series of assaults while she worked as a community carer for people with severe learning disabilities. Lisa, from Trafford, Greater Manchester, takes 16 different medicines and painkillers every day and has been unable to work since the late 1990s.

Her former employer, Trafford Healthcare NHS Trust, in Greater Manchester, agreed to the settlement just three weeks before the parties were due to go to court. It follows a ten-year battle for compensation over two particular assaults.

The mother-of-three said: "I was assaulted on a daily basis while working for the trust, as were many of the community carers.

"There was a chronic shortage of staff and I was not given any basic training or taught how to restrain patients. One of the houses, where four people lived and where I was assaulted, was the worst.

"I was repeatedly attacked and would come home with bite marks and bruises all over my body." Miss Carter was signed off work for ten months after the first major assault in 1996 and has not worked since the second assault in 1999.

She said: "I was told I wouldn't have to go back to that house but was sent on my first morning back at work. In the second assault, I was grabbed from behind, dragged to the floor by my hair and then stamped on and bitten.

"It caused permanent muscle and disc damage in my neck. I've lost about 50 percent of the movement in my right arm and have a dropped shoulder." The damage means Miss Carter cannot lift her arm properly or perform basic tasks, such as opening a window.

"The pain is constant and my cupboards are full of medication. I had hoped winning the case would help me get over it, but it hasn't, because the pain is still there."

Manchester-based law firm Rowlands Solicitors LLP acted on Miss Carter's behalf, and the trust accepted liability for the injuries in 2002. The settlement includes compensation for the debilitating injuries, her loss of earnings and her future care costs.

A trust spokesman said, "We are truly sorry for the injuries this lady sustained and would like to offer her our sincere apologies. We take our responsibilities as an employer very seriously and continually review the systems we have in place to ensure staff enjoy a safe working environment.

Sheila Costello, of Rowlands, said, "Her injuries were so severe that she still suffers pain daily and, as a result, won't be able to work again."

Further reading for this chapter:

Dawes, M	*Understanding Reasonable Force*	Derwent Press, 2006
Ashworth, A	*Principles of Criminal Law*	Oxford University Press, 2003
Herring, T	*Criminal Law*	Macmillan, 2010
Martin, J	*Key Cases Criminal Law*	Hodder Education, 2011
Bingham, T	*The Rule of Law*	Penguin, 2011

Chapter 9:

Behavioural Personal Safety

Case Study for this section:

In 2003, a 17-year old young woman walking a short distance home, alone, was abducted by a man driving a van. It is still unclear how he managed to get her into the vehicle, however within moments, terrified but using her considerable wits and intelligence, she was putting a variety of "passive" strategies into place.

She began by telling the man her name, and seems to have been telling him that she was just 15 (too young to have sexual intercourse with him legally). These are strategies which both make it hard for him to 'other' her, and also which begin to make her a high-risk target for inappropriate sexual advances. She also complies with his requests to keep her head down out of view. She answered his questions about where she was from, where she lived. Good passive strategies.

She also covertly accessed her mobile phone and managed to dial 999. The call connected with emergency services, and the system began recording the audio coming down the line from her handset as it sped through the streets, away from her home and towards the sparsely-populated countryside.

That's how we know what happened in the car. Unfortunately, she was never able to tell us herself what happened. In a stomach-churning failure of the system she thought she could rely on, the 999 system receiving the call hung up on her. The system failed to confirm an active caller on the other end of the phone. The system thought it was a wrong number, because there seemed to be no-one answering the operator's questions. It hung up the call.

Three days later, the young woman's body was found by a road-side. She had been abducted and held by a man for a period of about four hours, during which time he raped her and then killed her because she could identify him afterwards.

Her mother, waking to find her daughter's bedroom door wide open, began phoning her mobile at 5.30 am the next morning.

Six years later, the man was caught, prosecuted and convicted of the young woman's abduction, rape and murder, and received a life sentence in the UK. Part of the evidence against him was the phone call and recording she had made in the first few moments of the abduction, before the call was cut out.

Questions for Discussion:

1. **Why do Bad-Guys abduct people or move them from one place to another?**
2. **What place does negotiation / communication have in a scenario like this?**
3. **Is a violent fighting-back strategy an advisable one?**
4. **When should you absolutely fight? Is there a time when you should NOT fight?**
5. **Does fighting back make the bad-guy MORE dangerous to you?**
6. **Calling the authorities is a good idea. Who is ultimately responsible for your safety?**

The following 12 key points on personal safety have been collated from our research and experience of teaching general personal safety to clients on both a private and professional basis over many years. They represent a distillation of many key ideas, a summary of what may be the most important issues in staying safe while abroad in the community.

1: Behaviours which contribute to selection

Certain behaviours are correlated with the selection of victims. The victim's body language, posture, gait, environmental interaction, level of attention and pace are among the main factors which contribute to the selection matrix. If they are also "in the wrong place at the wrong time," somewhere isolated, where observation by others is poor, then the appraisal of the victim is likely to be of a "good target."

In the scientific field of "Victimology" there is a central concept called the "risk continuum" which insists that there are degrees of risk for a type of crime based on your career, lifestyle, relationships, movements and even personality—aspects which manifest themselves in your behaviour and demeanour. One researcher even studies a range of "exploitability" cues.

We are very quick to add that none of this means that victims are in any way responsible for the criminal acts that bad people may wish to carry out, merely that there is knowledge in the world about what elements of behaviour make one of those bad people select one of us for their attention. But by being aware of what subtle cues criminals look for, we can hopefully reduce the risk of becoming targets ourselves.

In a classic study, researchers Betty Grayson and Morris I. Stein asked convicted criminals to view a video of pedestrians walking down a busy New York City sidewalk, unaware they were being taped. The convicts had been to prison for violent offenses such as armed robbery, rape, and murder.

Within a few seconds, the convicts identified which pedestrians they would have been likely to target. What startled the researchers was that there was a clear consensus among the criminals about whom they would have picked as victims—and their choices were not based on gender, race, or age. Some petite, physically slight women were not selected as potential victims, while some large men were.

The researchers realized the criminals were assessing the ease with which they could overpower the targets based on several nonverbal signals—posture, body language, pace of walking, length of stride, and awareness of environment. Neither criminals nor victims were consciously aware of these cues. They are what psychologists call "precipitators," personal attributes that increase a person's likelihood of being criminally victimized.

The researchers analyzed the body language of the people on the tape, and identified several aspects of demeanor that marked potential victims as good targets. One of the main precipitators is a walking style that lacks "interactional synchrony" and "wholeness." Perpetrators notice a person whose walk lacks organized movement and flowing motion. Criminals view such people as less self-confident— perhaps because their walk suggests they are less athletic and fit— and are much more likely to exploit them.

http://www.psychologytoday.com/articles/200812/marked-mayhem

2: Trust your intuition

Intuitive feelings (cognitive dissonance) associate with interactions with others or with potentially threatening environments are often reliable clues to an impending violent incident or confrontation. Your brain will often work out when a trap is being sprung, or a predator is targeting you, or a situation is dangerous to you, long before your cognitive mind has worked out the problem. Act on feelings of discomfort.

Internationally renowned and respected violence prediction and threat assessment expert Gavin DeBecker says that "eerie feeling" is exactly what he wants people to pay attention to. *"We're trying to analyze the warning signs, and what I really want to teach...is that the feeling is the warning sign. All the other stuff is our explanation for the feeling. Why it was this, why it was that. The feeling itself is the warning sign."*

3: Refuse to be nice

Many of the worst asocial violence crimes are committed in places that are away from other human beings. Time alone with an attacker, away from other people, is associated with higher levels of violence and lower survival rates for the victim. Make all possible attempts to prevent your being moved from one location to another one. Refuse this, completely.

Rory Miller, from his excellent book, *Facing Violence*:

"The Process Predator requires time and privacy for what he intends to do... he will try to move the victim to another place with more privacy and security. This is called a secondary crime scene. It is very, very bad. There is no good outcome from a violent criminal wanting to spend private time with you."

"The fact that he is attempting to move you to a secondary crime scene...is a solid indicator that you are probably dealing with a process predator... Any risk to escape is worth the price. Get out of there."

189

Don't even talk to strangers on the street in isolated locations. One warning sign that you may be about to be robbed or attacked is the approach of a stranger on the street. The person may try to engage you in conversation. He may ask for the time, directions, bus fare, or try to tell you about a nice club or restaurant just around the corner. This is the classic "Distraction" method of mugging. Your best defense is—don't engage.

Don't be afraid to seem rude, abrupt or cold, either.

Gavin DeBecker states, *"I have not heard of one case in my entire career where someone was raped or murdered because they weren't nice. In other words, that's not the thing that motivates rape and murder. But I've heard of many, many cases where someone was victimized because they were open to the continued conversation with someone they didn't feel good about talking to."*

4: Be Hard Work

The more "professional" crimes are committed within what the perpetrator has accepted to be a favourable risk/reward /workload appraisal. Effective strategies for preventing these crimes include altering the perpetrator's appraisal of the factors they have included in their calculation. If you heighten risk, reduce reward and increase workload, you may tilt the balance in your favour.

"If I had the slightest inkling that a woman wasn't someone I could easily handle, then I would pass right on by. Or if I thought I couldn't control the situation, then I wouldn't even mess with the house, much less attempt a rape there," says Brad Morrison, a convicted sex offender who raped 75 women in 11 states.

Predators: Who They Are and How to Stop Them
—Gregory M. Cooper, Michael R. King, and Thomas McHoes.

You can escalate the risk to the attacker by fighting back (see point 12), or by moving slower than he needs you to (lengthening his exposure time to onlookers), or by calling for help, or by convincing them that help is already coming.

You can achieve a reduction in reward by convincing them that you don't have what they are looking for in terms of cash, valuables, sexual availability or desirability, or that you actually have much more in common with them than they thought (countering the resentment motive for some crimes). If you don't have what they want, they may discard you as a target.

A female client of mine, in her forties and with a young child at home, travels abroad on frequent business trips all over Europe, on her own, as a sales manager for a large corporation. At dinner by herself or in a hotel bar, she sometimes has interactions with men who are flirtatious, and sometimes persistent with their attentions. She is careful to send clear messages that she is unavailable, while being as courteous as the situation allows. Like most people, she resists being rude and prefers, where possible, a less-direct strategy when dealing with the more persistent men who don't hear her indirect "No." On one occasion, she spontaneously produced a flirtation-stopper: "I'm in town for a few days for my chemo-therapy." At this, the man's attention abruptly turned away from her, and she was left to return to her book.

You can increase workload by slowing things down, by introducing unknown factors into the scenario that he needs to work around ("the safe is on a time-lock!" "My cards have been cancelled!") and by generally being as troublesome a victim as he has met in his career as a mugger.

Of course, *if you feel it is safe to do so*, then give them what they want and stay alert until they leave you alone. This strategic submissiveness is important; consider that in gang/street violence, sometimes the violence is not used to coerce or to dominate the victim for their possessions alone; sometimes it is used to heighten the attacker's status within their group. Whether or not you hand over your valuables, this type of attacker may still use violence. If your intuition says to "leave it go" then submit strategically.

5: Use your body language intelligently

Some studies have found, classically, that as much as 90% of the content flying around within a conversation is transmitted through non-verbal means: Tone, Pitch, Pace, Volume and of course Body Motion (leaning, looking, turning, shifting and what your hands are doing).

Consider that the distance between people involved in a conversation can have a powerful effect on the emotional states they experience! Imagine someone who repeatedly breaches your personal space during an interaction. Whether that is for a good reason (you wanted them to be closer, such as in an intimate moment) or for a bad reason (you didn't want them to be near you, such as in a heated confrontation), either way it likely fires off powerful signals to your threat/reward system.

In our courses, we teach a very specific and refined model of body-language usage that we call Barrier Signals. We teach our attendees how to use Barrier Signals to control Proximity, Safety and Escape Route availability.

This method is a very sophisticated way of teaching people how to actively use their body language to stay safe during a confrontation. Curiously, this topic has huge depth to it and is massively important for the initial stages of a potentially violent encounter.

Most Breakaway and Self-Defence training courses actually skip or move through this phase very quickly; however, it is our experience that during this phase of the confrontation—when the attacker is moving through his pre-assault behaviours—that the intelligent use of body language is most critical to successful protection.

During this stage, there are many opportunities to slow down and prevent a successful violent assault—don't miss them! It is an unfortunate but humourous point to note that most self-defence instructors start at the worst possible moment of the incident (when the hair grab, the headlock or the bear hug is accomplished). In the timeline of a physical assault, there can be opportunities before this critical moment when an alert and motivated person can intercept the attacker's movement. Earlier intervention makes your escape easier than if you wait.

The result of our training is someone who presents assertive, but not submissive or aggressive, body language during a negotiation. Sometimes, depending on the type of negotiation, Aggressive (e.g. finger pointing/finger baton) or Submissive (e.g. Surrender Posture) modalities are what is called for; however, the baseline you need to understand is the Barrier/Negotiation signal (both hands in front of your body, palms towards the other person in a relaxed frame).

"A person with assertive body language is less likely to be chosen as a target for assault or exploitation."

Body Language and Assault Prevention:
A Review of the Literature

—Brad Binder, Ph.D.

Strategic Submissiveness

In some circumstances, body language may be manipulated by the victim to create opportunities for pro-actively defending themselves if and when an opportunity presents itself.

A "victim" who is ready to defend themselves may to all outwards appearances present the expected signs of someone who is intimidated and responsive to being pushed around; however, under the outward appearance of this veil of fear a well-prepared person may be actively processing opportunities for fighting back and escaping. We sometimes call this mind-set the "poisoned chalice" approach, and we teach it to our learners.

This "poisoned chalice" strategy is based on the element of surprise. The bad guy who carefully selects you, using the cues mentioned in Point 1 above, doesn't believe you will fight back (see Point 4). He has selected you because he believes he can shock, overpower and dominate you *easily*. If your behaviour convinces him of the success of his selection, then he will be relatively more relaxed when you execute your "Shock and Awe" defence.

As you fight back ferociously, you alter his target appraisal (Risk/Reward/Workload) and psychologically push the attacker out of their comfort zone. See point 12.

6: Understand what drives the Bad Guy

"Normal" people (those who are not professionally, biological-ly or habitually violent) use aggression or violence rarely and as an act of duress in the pursuit of one of the following:

1. To support or enhance their **Importance** within a group
2. To enforce **Stability** upon their circumstances
3. To have a sense of **Control** over you and their environment,
4. They perceive that you threaten their (or their group's) safety (you are a "Foe"/"Alien"/"Enemy") because
5. You have treated them (or represent a situation which has treated them) **Unfairly**.

According to some sources, these five domains (see the SCARF model in our chapter on communication strategies) represent the most powerful social drivers which influence human behaviour. In addition to the main survival-based behavioural influencers deep down in the primal brain, which drive us away from physical threats and towards physical rewards, these domains act as the emotional guides to a "successful" life.

Essentially, if:

1. You have a high status amongst your peers
2. Your life circumstances are stable and predictable
3. You have lots of control and therefore choice about how you live
4. You are surrounded by people you know well and feel safe with
5. Every negotiation you have is an equitable one

...then you are probably one of the happiest, most secure people in the world! It is when these five domains are threatened that we begin to feel stressed: our brain begins to work on the problems in an urgent way and demands that they are "fixed, NOW!" Hence, the descent to aggression.

Your efforts to defuse a situation should focus on these five domains:

1. Offer **Respect**, provide them a way to save "face"
2. **Clarify** details and explain rules, offer genuine, dependable advice
3. Give the person choices, alternatives and a sense of **Agency**
4. Establish two-way empathy, develop **Rapport** so that they feel safer with you
5. Make sure there is some give-and-take with **Reciprocity**

7: Be Ready to Be Decisive

Every person has the right to use "Reasonable Force" to protect themselves, if they honestly and reasonably believe it is necessary for them to do so and they have no means of withdrawing from the conflict. Reasonable force, if necessary, also requires that the force used is proportionate in the circumstances, causing no more harm than the risk of harm presented to the person by the situation.

When you listen to a news story on the television about a situation where force was used—such as in a home invasion, or in a bar-brawl, or in a controversial police action—then use it as an opportunity to exercise your own decision-making skills. Use the principles set out in our previous chapter to work out how you would respond, what factors would influence your decision and what actions you think would be necessary and proportionate in the circumstances.

Don't forget to think about the emotional content of the fight in question; how you might feel in a given situation will decide to a large extent your actions.

One issue we cover with our training attendees is about how far they believe they would be willing to go in order to protect themselves or a loved one from imminent violence. We sometimes describe very emotional scenarios and then ask the attendees what actions they would be prepared to take:

- Could you grab a knife and use it?
- Could you hit someone over the head with a heavy object?
- Could you push your thumb into someone's eye?

Depending on the scenario, people have different answers to this question, and it reveals the widely different wiring and conditioning in regards to violence that people have.

It is not important to me whether you think one way or the other about the level of violence you are ready to employ, but it might be important to you one day to know the extent of your feelings about using violence.

8: Make friends with your Own Monster

The threat of imminent personal harm will cause the body-mind system to kick in to high gear—a sudden release of survival hormones which prepare the body to run or to fight.

"More than anything else in life, it is the potential for intentional, overt, human confrontation that has the greatest ability to modify and influence the behaviour of human beings."

- Lt. Col. Dave Grossman, On Combat

The most immediate effect of this dumping of hormones into the system is an increase in heart rate and numerous sensations in the body and mind: a heightened state of consciousness paired with Olympic-athlete levels of strength and endurance—the release of the Monster inside them!

One of the results of the physical sensations associated with this change is that people think their body is going to pieces on them. Their internal monologue starts to drive negative thoughts.

"My legs are going to jelly! My tummy is doing somersaults and I feel like vomiting! My eyesight is gone all blurry! I'm dizzy and the ground is moving under me! My mouth is dry and my voice feels funny! I'm cold! Oh God, I'm falling to pieces!"

These reactions to the biological signs of fear are perfectly natural; however, they aren't very helpful! Luckily with a little help, they can be reversed and become positively anchored. Imagine a world-class athlete at the starting line for a race as the time draws near for the starting gun to fire. The winners are not thinking about how the other runners are going to be faster than them; they are focussed on channelling all of their nervous energies towards achieving their goal! When the starting gun fires, they release the Monster to do its work!

The internal monologue should then become:

"There go my legs, ready for the run! My stomach is tightening—energy pooling there! My eyes are focussing—only on important things. I'm starting to float—lighter, faster. No need for talking now—think! Cooling—ready! R_E_A_D_Y!"

9: Keep Your Monster on a Leash

Over-arousal can cause negative effects: if a person's heart rate elevates rapidly without control or awareness in a novel situation, this can often result in reduced performance in cognitive tasks and complex motions. Keep it *simple* when planning a physical movement or developing a plan. Remember, your body is trying to help you!

Another aspect of keeping the Monster on a leash is that, by definition, the Monster has different standards of behaviour. It has broader limits to which it will extend in order to protect you. So many people end up standing in front of magistrates on Monday mornings all over the UK because they released the monster on Saturday night because of a spilled pint or a wrong-glance. The Monster—and its well-known favourite tipple, the "Red Mist"—can be responsible for survival at the cost of liberty.

The trick with your Monster is knowing when to release it from its tether, allowing it enough reach to meet its objectives, but restraining it against pursuing the objective too far. Training can help with this, especially with drills and exercises which teach the different decision-making and scenario/engagement principles which are needed.

10: Be a good Coach (to yourself)

It is easy to become emotionally overloaded in a situation which is unfamiliar. For most people, being in a physical assault scenario is completely novel and utterly unpleasant experience. Biological/physical overload as described above is often accompanied by negative self-talk, attributions or limiting beliefs:

"I can't do this! Women can't defend themselves against men! What if he hits me and the injury is disfiguring? He's bigger than me! Is it going to hurt? I don't want to hurt anyone! I KNEW this would happen!"

Negative self-talk will beat you into the ground long before the Bad Guy ever will! Try to consider these self-limiting beliefs NOW.

"The whole thing is never to get negative about yourself. Sure, it's possible that the other guy you're playing is tough and that he may have beaten you the last time you played, and okay, maybe you haven't been playing all that well yourself. But the minute you start thinking about these things, you're dead. I go out to every match convinced that I'm going to win. That's all there is to it."

Athlete's Comments
Foundations of Sport and Exercise Psychology
Weinberg & Gould

Remember: with stress it is the negative appraisal of the external demand which triggers the challenge to the system's coping resources. Re-appraisal of situation (a re-framing of the picture, so to speak) can help to combat this negative spiralling effect.

Developing positive self-talk during a conflict scenario can be a hugely powerful ally. Often it can be your instructor's voice which repeats and repeats in your head the time-won advice to "Get UP, NOW!" or to "Keep your hands UP."

One of the most powerful ways to get your Monster moving in the right direction is to give it something to move towards—your Survival Anchor.

11: Throw yourself a Survival Anchor

Many people who overcome their attackers do so because in the midst of their confrontation they find a survival anchor and throw it into their near future. Often it is the thought of seeing their family when they get home. Think about your survival anchor and have it ready!

In 2007, a 33-year old market researcher visited the flat of Gordon Melrose in Edinburgh. Melrose (59) was known to local criminal justice and social care professionals, as he was a known sex-offender, having served a total of 18 years for assaults and sex attacks. When the market researcher visited him at home, he offered her his cooperation in the survey and a seat on his sofa.

Moments later as she finished her survey and packed away her things, Melrose pushed her onto the sofa, presented a knife and, holding his hand over her mouth, began threatening her.

In a key moment, the woman made a decision to fight back. She began to struggle against him and scream. Melrose: "Undress! Undress or I kill you!"

The woman describes how this crystallised her thoughts: "I have to live." An incredible thing must have happened, as the world rotated around that knife for a moment, because the woman emerged from it with a plan: she would fight and she would escape!

Struggling under his weight, she grabbed a coffee mug lying on a nearby table and smashed it into Melrose's head, opening up gashes that later needed stitches. He dropped the knife, which she scooped up. She dived under a dining table, clinging to the knife, with Melrose punching her as she sought sanctuary there.

The minutes that followed are straight out of an action movie. At one point she pulled down an aquarium full of tropical fish in an effort to slow Melrose as he chased her around the flat. Eventually the police, called by neighbours, arrived and a police dog took Melrose down. He later needed 15 stitches in the head wound the woman had given him.

What made this woman into a survivor? How did she take on a man who was much larger than her and win? How did she take the knife from him? How did she overcome the shock and move with her indignation? Why didn't she acquiesce and allow herself to be intimidated?

In an interview later, the woman revealed what had fuelled and motivated her to do battle with this experienced, committed sex predator. "I begged him not to do it because I have got two children to live for."

The reasons why many other supposed victims turn their scenarios around, lies in where they place their focus at the critical moment.

We often note that, "It's not what you fight with, but what you fight *for* that matters."

Ironically, most people we meet will think twice about hurting someone else in defence of themselves, mainly because it means that they might get into trouble and ruin their lives if the legal aftermath turns against them. The irony is that, if they hesitate to act, then they may not be alive to go back to work tomorrow, or they may not have the psychological or physical resources needed to go back to work after such an incident.

The Survival Anchor is an image, a feeling or any kind of embodiment of those things which we will be powerfully drawn towards during a crisis. It's a grappling hook to climb over a wall. It's a life raft in a hurricane and an anchor in stormy seas. What is your Survival Anchor?

12: Bring it all together and Just Do It!

Negotiation and de-escalation should always be your first option in terms of dealing with aggressive behaviour. As we have seen though, there is a point where the aggressor's behaviour crosses a line and the probability that you can talk your way out of being victimised virtually disappears as the spiral turns tighter and tighter.

Research has shown that in these circumstances, fighting back hard and fast, with the best ferocity and indignation you can muster, massively increases your chance of stopping any victimisation from progressing further.

Even in a situation where you make an attempt to protect yourself like this, and despite your efforts you are not wholly successful, any decision you have taken to make a stand against the aggressor in defence of yourself will psychologically assist your recovery in the aftermath of an event.

Your best chance will come when you have mustered your ferocity and indignation and you take action fuelled by your Survival Anchor. Action like this has the best chance of facilitating your escape from most situations, especially coupled with the surprise element mentioned in point 5.

"A number of studies find that several active resistance strategies are effective for avoiding rape without increasing risk of physical injury."

Further reading for this chapter:

Miller, R	*Meditations on Violence*	YMAA, 2008
Snortland, E	*Beauty Bites Beast*	B3 Books, 1998
Cooper, G and King, M	*Predators - Who they are and how to stop them*	Prometheus Books, 2007
Meichenbaum, D	*Stress Inoculation Training*	Pergamon Press, 1985

End Note

Well done! You have navigated your way through the vast swathe of different subjects which are encompassed within Lone Worker Personal Safety. Along the way we have learned valuable lessons from some tragic incidents—'Mortui Vivos Docent.'

We have looked at legal and regulatory issues for working alone, investigated the psychology of aggression and explored the physiology of stress. We have underlined the importance of using your intuition to inform your decisions and some of the motivation and resilience you may need to be street-smart. We have enabled you with knowledge about your legal rights to protect yourself physically and we have given the lone-worker safety device its rightful significance.

So, my hope for you now is that you will have some mature, adult conversations within your organisation about how to keep lone-workers safer. Address those systematic issues which will influence safety for the whole team. Shore-up the gaps in information and supervision that might exist.

Work more confidently with your clients, knowing that you understand the fundamental concerns which drive their behaviour. Respond flexibly and with that heightened awareness to defuse situations where your clients are becoming upset, frustrated or aggressive.

But if, with the vanishingly small chance that all of the above fails, and you need to physically remove yourself from a situation or protect yourself from violence, then you can proceed with the enablement of 'Reasonable Force.'

I hoped to give you an illuminating tour of the Alert, Preventive and Survival attitudes in this book. My wish is that now that we are finished our chat, you can resort to Attitude # 1: the Relaxed Attitude!

Bibliography

De Becker, G	*The Gift of Fear*	Bloomsbury, 1997
Braithwaite, R	*Managing Aggression*	Routledge, 2001
Maden, Tony MD MRCPsych	*Treating Violence*	Oxford University Press, 2007
Eagleman, D	*Incognito - The secret lives of our brain*	Canongate, 2011
Lehrer, J	*The Decisive Moment*	Canongate Books, 2009
Kahneman, D	*Thinking Fast and Slow*	Allen Lane Penguin, 2011
Klein, G	*Streetlights and Shadows: Searching for the Keys to Adaptive Decision Making*	MIT Press, 2009
Health and Safety Executive	"Five steps to risk assessment." INDG163	HSE
Health and Safety Executive	"Working alone: Health and safety guidance on the risks of lone working." (Leaflet INDG73)	HSE
Fox, B & Polkey, C & Boatman, P	*Managing Violence in the Workplace*	Tolley / Reed Elsevier, 2002
Paterson, B and Turnbull, J	*Aggression and Violence: Approaches to Effective Management*	Macmillan, 1999

Bibliography

Taylor, B	*Working with Aggression and Resistance in Social Work*	Learning Matters Ltd., 2011
Collins, S	*Health and Safety - Workbook for Social Care*	Jessica Kinglsey Publishers, 2009
Halstead, P	*Key Cases in Human Rights*	Hodder Education, 2009
Grossman, D	"On Combat - The Psychology and Physiology of Deadly Conflict in War and Peace"	PPCT Research Publications, 2004
Siddle, B	"Sharpening the Warrior's Edge"	PPCT Research Publications, 1995
Schmidt, R & Wrisberg, C	*Motor Learning And Performance*	Human Kinetics, 2008
Hancock, A and Szalma, J	*Performance Under Stress - Human Factors Series*	Ashgate, 2008
Klinger, D	*Into the Kill Zone*	Wiley, 2004
Morris, D	*The Human Zoo*	Vintage, 1994
Morris, D	*The Naked Ape*	Corgi Books, 1967
Morris, D	*Manwatching - A Field guide to Human Behaviour*	Grafton Books, 1997
Winston, R	*Human Instinct - How our primeval impulses shape our modern lives*	Bantam Books, 2002
Goleman, D	"Emotional Intelligence: Why it can matter more than IQ"	Bloomsbury, 1996

Thompson, G & Jenkins, J	*Verbal Judo - The Gentle Art of Persuasion*	Quill, 1993
Fisher, R & Ury, W	*Getting to Yes - Negotiating an Agreement Without Giving In*	Random House, 1981
Rock, D	"Your Brain at Work"	Harper Business, 2009
Rock, D	"SCARF: a brain-based model for collaborating with and influencing others"	www.neuroleadership.org, 2008
LeDoux, J	*The Emotional Brain*	Phoenix, 1998
Ekman, P	*Emotions Revealed - Understanding Faces and Feelings*	Phoenix, 2003
Thompson, G & Jenkins, J	*Verbal Judo - The Gentle Art of Persuasion*	Quill, 1993
Fisher, R & Ury, W	*Getting to Yes - Negotiating an Agreement Without Giving In*	Random House, 1981
Morris, D	*The Human Zoo*	Vintage, 1994
Morris, D	*The Naked Ape*	Corgi Books, 1967
Morris, D	*Manwatching - A Field guide to Human Behaviour*	Grafton Books, 1997
Ekman, P	*Emotions Revealed - Understanding Faces and Feelings*	Phoenix, 2003

Bibliography

Winston, R	*Human Instinct - How our primeval impulses shape our modern lives*	Bantam Books, 2002
Tallis, R	*Michelangelo's Finger*	Atlantic Books, 2010
Dawes, M	*Understanding Reasonable Force*	Derwent Press, 2006
Ashworth, A	*Principles of Criminal Law*	Oxford University Press, 2003
Herring, T	*Criminal Law*	Macmillan, 2010
Martin, J	*Key Cases Criminal Law*	Hodder Education, 2011
Bingham, T	*The Rule of Law*	Penguin, 2011
Miller, R	*Meditations on Violence*	YMAA, 2008
Snortland, E	*Beauty Bites Beast*	B3 Books, 1998
Cooper, G and King, M	*Predators - Who they are and how to stop them*	Prometheus Books, 2007
Meichenbaum, D	*Stress Inoculation Training*	Pergamon Press, 1985

www.ingramcontent.com/pod-product-compliance
Lightning Source LLC
Chambersburg PA
CBHW060501290526
45791CB00001B/209